Whole

Where Spiritual Alignment Meets Daily Life

A Guide to Healing What's Hidden and Living Authentically

IVORY JAMERSON

Whole: Where Spiritual Alignment Meets Daily Life - A Guide to Healing What's Hidden and Living Authentically

Copyright © 2025 by Ivory Jamerson
All rights reserved.

No part of this publication may be reproduced, stored in a retrieval system, or transmitted in any form or by any means—electronic, mechanical, photocopying, recording, or otherwise—without the prior written permission of the author, except for brief quotations used in reviews or scholarly works with proper citation.

Published by:
BeWhole Publishing
An imprint of Spiritual Healthcare Consulting
30 N Gould St Ste R
Sheridan, WY 82801
spiritualhealthcareconsulting.com

IMPORTANT NOTE TO READERS

This book has been written and published for informational and educational purposes only. It is not intended to serve as medical advice or as a substitute for any form of professional medical treatment.

Always consult with your physician before altering or changing any aspect of your health regimen. Do not discontinue or adjust prescription medications without guidance from a licensed medical provider. Any use of the information in this book is made at the reader's discretion and is the reader's sole responsibility.

This book does not diagnose, treat, or cure any medical conditions. It is not intended to replace the care of licensed healthcare professionals.

This book is independently authored and published. No sponsorship or endorsement by, nor affiliation with, any trademarked brands or products mentioned is claimed or implied. All trademarks belong to their respective owners and are used here solely for informational purposes. The author and publisher encourage readers to support the brands referenced in this book.

Dedication

To my husband, Chad —

We have been through it all.

The valleys and the victories. The breaking and the rebuilding.

Through every season, your love has remained.

Thank you for standing beside me, for believing in me,

and for building this life with me—brick by brick, prayer by prayer.

Together, we still stand.

And together, we rise.

This book is for you.

CONTENTS

Whole
My Definition

My Story
From Misalignment to Wholeness

Introduction
Why You Feel Misaligned (And Why You're Not Broken)

- The real reason you feel stuck, out of sync, and disconnected
- What spiritual alignment really means (without fluff or dogma)
- Why self-help hasn't worked—and what we're doing differently
- What "whole" really looks like: a life that feels like you, not a performance

---

Part I: Naming the Ache – Understanding Misalignment

Chapter 1: The Primary Complaint

- "I don't feel like myself"—dissecting the internal friction
- How misalignment shows up: anxiety, burnout, lack of fulfillment
- The cost of ignoring your truth: peace, progress, and purpose

Chapter 2: The False Self You've Been Performing

- How we learn to survive by becoming who we think we should be
- Masks, roles, and the burden of expectations
- The spiritual wound of disconnection

Chapter 3: Why Fixes Haven't Worked

- The limits of productivity, pop psychology, and positive thinking
- Why information alone doesn't create transformation
- The missing ingredient: integration and inner connection

Part II: Returning to Center – The Work of Reconnection

Chapter 4: Your Inner Compass – Values, Voice & Vision

- Rediscovering what actually matters to you
- Exercises: clarify your core values and non-negotiables
- Reclaiming the voice underneath the noise

Chapter 5: Healing What's Hidden

- Naming and nurturing the unhealed parts of you
- How trauma, shame, and spiritual wounds hijack alignment
- Practices from spiritual care: grief rituals, compassion exercises, embodied prayer

Chapter 6: Soul-Level Clarity in a World That Wants You Confused

- How culture, capitalism, and perfectionism keep you scattered
- Building sacred boundaries to protect your energy and focus
- Inner listening practices: how to hear yourself again

Part III: Becoming Whole – Alignment in Daily Life

Chapter 7: From Knowing to Becoming – Embodying the True Self

- The difference between awareness and embodiment
- Creating rhythms of alignment: spiritual disciplines for the real world
- Morning rituals, evening resets, and micro-alignments

Chapter 8: Inner Peace as a Practice, Not a Place

- Why peace isn't passive—it's courageous
- Releasing the inner critic and perfectionism
- Practices: breath prayers, stillness moments, somatic settling

Chapter 9: Building a Life That Feels Like You

- How to redesign your schedule, relationships, and goals from the inside out
- Life integration map: career, creativity, community, care
- What aligned decision-making actually looks like (practical model)

Part IV: The Becoming Never Ends – Staying Aligned as You Grow

Chapter 10: When You Outgrow Who You Were

- Normalizing identity shifts, growing pains, and spiritual evolution
- Letting go of roles and identities that no longer serve
- Grieving and celebrating your past selves

Chapter 11: Integration Over Perfection

- How to stay rooted when life gets loud again
- Embracing cyclical growth and spiritual maintenance
- Practices: monthly check-ins, seasonal resets, community reflection

Chapter 12: Living Authentically in Real Life

- Being whole in a fractured world
- What it looks like to walk in alignment even when others don't get it
- A final blessing: you don't have to hustle to be holy, or perfect to be whole

Closing

You Were Never Broken. You Were Just Disconnected

- You've always been whole—this journey just helped you remember

- Encouragement for the next chapter of your becoming

- Final integration exercise: a letter to your future aligned self

---

About the Author

Ivory Jamerson

- Spiritual Life - Social Life - Whole Life

- #ThatChaplain

- "Spiritual Care is Whole Care" - Ivory

Whole

The Definition

Whole - Living fully aligned in spirit, soul, and body. It's not about perfection, but about authenticity. Being whole means returning to who God created you to be, before the pressure, pain, and performance layered over your truth. It's peace in your pace, clarity in your choices, and freedom in your faith. It's living from the inside out—rooted, real, and reconciled with both God and yourself.

That's what this journey is about.
Not doing more. Not becoming someone else.
But remembering who you've always been beneath the noise.

My Story

From Misalignment to Wholeness

I didn't write this book from a pedestal. I wrote it from the valley.

There was a season in my life when I knew I was meant for more—but I couldn't see the way forward. I felt stuck, lost, weighed down by imposter syndrome and unworthiness. I was showing up for everyone else, but I was disconnected from myself.

My habits were inconsistent. My discipline was broken. I was overwhelmed by too much information and not enough wisdom. I was surrounded by people, yet felt alone and misunderstood. And the loudest voice I heard wasn't God's—it was my own inner critic, whispering sabotage: *You're failing. You're too much. You'll never get this right.*

I was out of sync with the real me.
And I was exhausted.

I've been married for over 20 years now—but when we began, we were just 19 and 20, with no road map, no mentors, and no clear direction. We learned marriage and ministry the hard way—through trial, tears, trauma and truth. We waited 16 long years to have children. In that waiting, I experienced four devastating miscarriages. I walked through grief that nearly crushed my soul.

Then one day, as I was pouring myself out in service, doing what I thought God had called me to do, someone I respected told me I was a failure. That I'd made too many mistakes. That I wasn't enough. On top of that, my marriage was failing, my home was crumbling, and my relationships suffered.

Something in me broke.

My health declined. My hope deflated. And all I had left—*was God*.

But that's where healing began.

God didn't discard me. He met me in the middle of my mess. He reminded me that I was created on purpose, with a purpose. That every flaw I carried was something He could work with—not something He needed to erase.

So I stopped trying to fix myself externally and started working on my **spiritual health**. And slowly, that inner work began to restore my **soul**—my mind, my will, and my emotions. From there, I began to see transformation in my **body**—my physical health, my energy, my strength. I wasn't just getting better. I was becoming *whole*.

Today, I am a mother of five beautiful children—including two teenagers who are teaching me new dimensions of love. I'm an entrepreneur in the work of spiritual care, counseling, coaching, and consulting. I am a missionary currently serving the community of Oyugis in Kenya, Africa, I am a clinical chaplain, a senior leader in ministry, a spiritual counselor, and a friend.

I have my Master of Divinity. I'm in the final phase of my Master of Social Work and a member of **Alpha Chi National College Honor Society**, top 10% of my class. I've served as a hospice chaplain, an addiction and recovery chaplain, and a community chaplain. I founded two spiritual healthcare centers that integrate care for the **spirit, soul, and body**. And I've walked with hundreds of people in the most sacred spaces of their pain, their calling, and their healing.

I've lived this message.

I wrote this book for people like you—people who are tired of pretending, tired of performing, and ready to live a life that feels *like them* again. People who want to grow but feel stuck. People who have dreams but wrestle with doubt. People who love God but feel far from themselves.

If that's you, I want you to know something:

You are not broken. You are not behind. You are not too late.

You are on the edge of something holy.
And this book is your invitation to come home—to yourself, to your Creator, and to the life you were always meant to live.

You're not just going to read *WHOLE*.
You're going to *walk it*.
You're going to embody it.
And with God's help, you're going to become someone even you didn't know was possible.

Let's begin this journey—together.

Introduction: Why You Feel Misaligned (And Why You're Not Broken)

You may not be able to put it into words, but something inside you knows:
This isn't me.
You're functioning, showing up, getting through your days—but under the surface, there's a quiet ache. A subtle grief. A sense that you're living just slightly off-center.

You're not alone.

I've sat with women and men, children and teens, leaders and caregivers, professionals and pastors, mothers and mentors—all of them quietly asking the same question:
Why do I feel so out of sync with myself?

They're not lazy. They're not faithless. They're not broken.
And neither are you.

What you're experiencing is **misalignment**—a disconnection between the life you're living and the truth of who you are. It doesn't always scream.
Sometimes it whispers.
Through burnout.
Through anxiety.
Through resentment.
Through a weariness that rest doesn't fix.

This book is about that ache. And the invitation it offers.

The Real Reason You Feel Stuck, Out of Sync, and Disconnected

So many of us have spent years performing who we thought we needed to be—shaped by trauma, expectation, or survival. We became adaptable, impressive, responsible, spiritual. But in the process, we slowly drifted from our *center*.

Maybe you can relate.

Maybe you know what to say but not how to feel.
Maybe you've been leading while quietly losing yourself.
Maybe you've mastered the art of showing up while slowly shutting down.

But here's the truth: **you're not broken. You're just disconnected.**

Disconnection feels like fragmentation. You're one version of yourself at work, another at home, another in your career, and still another in your own head. But wholeness—that's where peace lives. That's where clarity lives. That's where you come back to life.

What Spiritual Alignment Really Means (Without Fluff or Dogma)

Spiritual alignment isn't about religion or rituals. It's about living from the inside out—when your spirit, soul, and body begin moving in the same direction.

As I shared in the beginning of this book, I define **whole** like this:

> *Whole means living fully aligned in spirit, soul, and body. It's not about perfection, but about authenticity. Being whole means returning to who God created you to be, before the pressure, pain, and performance layered over your truth. It's peace in your pace, clarity in your choices, and freedom in your faith. It's living from the inside out—rooted, real, and reconciled with both God and yourself.*

Wholeness doesn't mean life gets easy. It means *you get anchored*.
It means you stop living from pressure and start living from *presence*.

Why Self-Help Hasn't Worked—and What We're Doing Differently

You've probably tried to "fix" this feeling before—read the devotionals, bought the planners, downloaded the apps, told yourself to push through. But insight without integration leads to exhaustion. Information alone doesn't change you.

That's why this isn't a self-help book.
This is a **soul-help journey**.

In these pages, we're not just talking about truth—we're *living* it. Together.
You'll explore the hidden sources of misalignment.
You'll learn spiritual and emotional practices that reconnect you to yourself and to God.
You'll slow down enough to listen to the voice beneath the noise.

And most importantly—you'll stop performing and start *embodying*.

What "Whole" Really Looks Like: A Life That Feels Like You

Being whole doesn't mean being fixed. It means being *faithful*—to your design, your values, your God.

It looks like:

- A schedule that reflects your priorities—not your pressure.

- Boundaries that protect your peace—not walls built from fear.

- Habits that feel like nourishment—not punishment.

- A presence that feels *real*—not rehearsed.

A whole life feels like *you* again. Not the version who's always on. Not the one who needs to earn belonging. But the one who is already *worthy*, already *loved*, and finally *home*.

How to Walk This Journey

Each chapter in this book will guide you through:

- **Inner Exploration** – to uncover what's hidden

- **Spiritual Practices** – to restore alignment

- **Practical Application** – to integrate what you're learning

- **Reflective Journaling** – because healing is not just read, it's *lived*

You can go chapter by chapter or linger where your soul feels drawn. This is your journey—and the pace is sacred.

Note To Reader

The stories and personal examples shared in this book are intended for illustrative and educational purposes only. While inspired by real-life experiences, all names, identifying details, and circumstances have been changed or fictionalized to protect the privacy and confidentiality of individuals.

Any resemblance to actual persons, living or deceased, is purely coincidental.

This book is not intended to serve as a substitute for professional therapy, medical advice, or professional counseling. If you are experiencing emotional or mental health challenges, please seek support from a healthcare professional.

Before We Begin...

Take a deep breath.

You don't have to strive your way into this work.
You don't have to prove that you're ready.
You don't have to be perfect.

You are already enough.
You are already seen.
And you are already being called back to yourself.

Let this book be a soft place to land.
A brave place to uncover.
And a sacred place to *return*.

Let's begin.

Section 1: Naming the Ache – Understanding Misalignment

Chapter 1: The Primary Complaint

"I don't feel like myself."

As a clinical chaplain, I've heard this phrase more times than I can count. It comes in quiet whispers and through tears. It rises up in frustration and spills out in exhaustion. It's one of the most honest confessions a person can make—one that holds sacred weight. And whenever I hear it, I listen closely. Because it's not just a statement. It's a signal. A holy invitation.

People don't usually arrive at this moment quickly. It's not typically the result of one bad day or even one hard season. More often, it's a gradual drift—subtle and slow. It begins with little compromises, a few emotional numbing mechanisms, and the ever-growing pressure to perform, succeed, or simply survive.

You keep going because life demands it. You show up for your family. You fulfill your responsibilities. You check the boxes, say the right things, do what's expected of you. On the outside, everything may even look fine. But somewhere along the way, the connection to your truest self begins to dim.

You don't recognize yourself in the mirror like you used to. Your joy feels muted. Your laughter, rare. Your thoughts are noisy, but your soul is silent. You're present, but not connected. You're functioning, but not flourishing.

Something feels off—and you can't quite name it.

I want to tell you what I tell the people who sit across from me in counseling or spiritual care sessions when they say those exact words:

You are not broken.

This dissonance you feel isn't a sign of your failure—it's a sign of your *faithfulness*. You've held so much for so long, often without help. You've endured, adjusted, and adapted. But now, something in you is asking for more. Not more effort, not more pressure—but more *truth*. More *authenticity*. More *alignment*.

That longing is not a problem to be fixed. It's a whisper from God, inviting you back to yourself.

The Warning Signs of Disconnection

Most people can't pinpoint the exact moment they stopped feeling like themselves. It sneaks in subtly, disguised as stress, fatigue, or disinterest. But over time, the signs grow louder:

- **You feel like you're just going through the motions.**

- **You no longer enjoy the things that used to bring you life.**

- **You're quick to anger or tears, and you don't know why.**

- **You feel guilty for needing rest, silence, or solitude.**

- **You crave escape—from your job, your responsibilities, even yourself.**

These symptoms aren't just emotional—they're spiritual. They reveal a fracture between the image you present and the essence of who you are. And when your soul is out of sync with your identity, life begins to feel heavy.

When Your Inner World Doesn't Match Your Outer Life

At one point in my own journey, I was pouring out in ministry and in my community, speaking on stages, mentoring others, and showing up for my family. And yet, in the quiet moments, I felt hollow. I questioned whether I was truly walking in purpose or simply playing a role.

My discipline was broken. My habits were inconsistent. My mind was racing with information, but I lacked wisdom. I was surrounded by people, yet I felt alone—misunderstood, even invisible. The loudest voice I heard wasn't God's voice of grace. It was my own inner critic whispering sabotage: *You're too much. You're not enough. You're failing. You'll never get it right.*

That voice doesn't just discourage you—it distorts you. It pushes you into hyper-productivity or paralyzing procrastination. It makes you question your worth and withdraw from the very relationships that could help you heal. It makes you feel like a stranger in your own life.

But here's the truth I had to learn—and the one I now share with others:

> When you feel furthest from yourself, you're often closest to a breakthrough.

A Holy Disruption

There is something sacred about the moment you admit, *"I don't feel like myself."* It may seem like defeat, but it's actually the beginning of deliverance. It's the moment when the performance starts to fall away, and what remains is a soul that's ready to be seen.

I believe God meets us most powerfully in these moments—not with condemnation, but with compassion. He doesn't demand we have it all figured out. He simply asks us to come home.

Home to the truth of who we are. Home to the healing we've avoided. Home to the grace we've needed all along.

Realignment Begins Within

We live in a world obsessed with external solutions—self-help strategies, productivity hacks, appearance upgrades, and lifestyle overhauls. But real transformation doesn't start with your schedule, your goals, or your habits. It starts with your soul.

When I began to heal, I didn't start with my diet, my workout routine, or my time management. I started by tending to the parts of me I had neglected—my grief, my fear, my weariness. I returned to spiritual practices that helped me listen again—prayer, stillness, journaling, scripture. I gave myself permission to feel without judgment, to rest without guilt, to be without performing.

Slowly, I began to reconnect with myself. And as I did, something shifted. My energy returned. My focus sharpened. My emotions stabilized. I wasn't just coping. I was coming alive.

The same can be true for you.

The Courage to Be Honest

One of the most courageous things you can do is tell the truth about where you are. Not the curated truth. Not the polished version. But the honest, vulnerable truth that says:

- "I'm tired of pretending."
- "I miss the person I used to be."
- "I want to feel joy again."
- "I'm not okay—and that's okay."

That honesty creates space for healing. It allows you to stop striving and start surrendering. It gives God something to work with. Not the mask, not the performance—but *you*.

And here's what's beautiful: when you begin to reconnect with yourself, you also begin to reconnect with God. Because He doesn't dwell in the fantasy version of your life. He meets you in the truth of it.

Permission to Come Back to Life

Sometimes we need someone to give us permission. So let me say this to you clearly and compassionately:

You have permission to stop performing. You have permission to ask for help. You have permission to rest. You have permission to grieve what you've lost. You have permission to hope again.

More than that, **you have permission to become who you really are.**

Wholeness Is the Goal

The aim of this book is not perfection—it's *wholeness*. That means honoring all parts of who you are: your spirit, your soul, and your body. It means listening to your needs instead of ignoring them. It means bringing your whole self into your relationship with God, not just the "holy" parts.

Wholeness is about alignment. When your inner world—your values, beliefs, desires, and identity—aligns with your outer life, you experience a deep sense of peace. That's what it means to "feel like yourself" again.

You were created in the image of a whole and holy God. And that means your healing is not only possible—it's promised. But it won't come through more hustle. It comes through *honesty*, *intimacy with God*, and *intentional alignment*.

Your Soul is Speaking

So if you've found yourself saying, "I don't feel like myself," I want to invite you to lean in. Don't rush past this moment. Don't minimize it or silence it. Listen. Your soul is speaking. Your soul is your mind, your will and your emotions. Your soul is housed in your heart and out of the heart according to Proverbs 4:23, flows the issues of life.

Your soul is asking for truth. It's asking for rest. It's asking for healing. It's asking for home.

This is your sacred invitation to return to yourself, to re-center in God's presence, and to realign your life from the inside out.

You are not too far gone. You are not too late. You are not too broken.

You're just out of sync. And you're being lovingly invited back into alignment.

The Friction Within: What Misalignment Feels Like

Misalignment isn't always loud. It often shows up in whispers:

- An unshakable anxiety, even when everything looks "fine"

- Burnout from carrying responsibilities that no longer bring meaning

- A lack of fulfillment, despite achieving your goals

- A sense of distance from God, others, or yourself
- Inner criticism that feels constant and cruel
- Irritability or emotional numbness you can't explain

These aren't just bad habits or poor time management. They are **indicators**—sacred symptoms pointing to something deeper: a disconnection between your *inner world* and your *outer life*.

Misalignment happens when we live in a way that no longer reflects who we truly are or what we deeply believe. It often develops over time, shaped by unspoken expectations, survival patterns, or seasons of trauma. The result? We live outside of our truth. We perform instead of connect. We survive instead of thrive.

But here's the good news: just as misalignment happened gradually, realignment can begin moment by moment, with grace.

The Cost of Ignoring Your Truth

When we ignore our truth, the consequences are subtle at first, then cumulative. Over time, the cost becomes clear:

- We lose our **peace**, because we're constantly managing pressure
- We lose our **progress**, because we're busy but not aligned
- We lose our **purpose**, because we've forgotten who we really are

And perhaps most painfully—we lose connection with ourselves.

But here's what I want you to know: **you can return.** You can reconnect. And you don't have to earn your way back to wholeness. You simply need to begin by telling the truth—first to yourself, and then to God.

Inner Exploration: Alignment Self-Check

Take a few moments of quiet reflection. With gentleness, respond to the following statements. Rate each from 1 (Strongly Disagree) to 5 (Strongly Agree):

1. I feel at peace with who I am and how I'm living.

2. I can express my needs without guilt or fear.

3. My daily life reflects my deepest values and beliefs.

4. I have energy and motivation to show up fully each day.

5. I experience joy and fulfillment consistently.

6. I feel connected to God in a way that's life-giving, not performative.

7. I'm not driven by fear of failure or the need to prove myself.

8. I trust myself to make decisions that align with my truth.

Reflection Questions:

1. When was the last time you truly felt like yourself?

2. What areas of your life feel out of alignment right now?

3. What are the habits, people, or pressures that may be contributing to your sense of disconnection?

4. What might it look like to give yourself permission to rest, realign, and reconnect?

5. What is one small practice you can begin today to move toward wholeness?

Don't rush through this. Let this check-in become a sacred space of clarity and compassion.

Practical Tools: Gentle Steps Toward Realignment

You don't need to fix everything overnight. Begin with one shift, one small act of alignment.

1. Morning Alignment Check-In

Before checking your phone or diving into your to-do list, ask:

- *How am I feeling—spiritually, emotionally, physically?*

- *What do I need today to feel more grounded and connected to God?*

2. Truth Journaling (10 minutes)

Ask yourself:

- *What truth am I avoiding?*

- *What is one small way I can honor that truth today?*

3. Embodied Stillness

Sit in silence for 5 minutes. Close your eyes. Breathe deeply.
Gently say: *"I am safe to return to myself. God meets me here."*

Let your nervous system begin to associate stillness with safety—not pressure.

4. Weekly Alignment Review

At the end of the week, reflect:

- *What choices brought me peace?*

- *What drained me or pulled me out of alignment?*

- *What do I want to shift in the coming week?*

Maya's Wake-Up Call

Maya was a mother of three, active in church and her community, and always available for everyone—except herself. "I'm tired of pretending I'm okay," she told me. She wasn't battling sin—she was battling silence. She had been ignoring her truth for years, afraid it would cost her everything.

But when Maya began to gently honor what was real—through journaling, soul care, and courageous conversations—she didn't fall apart. She finally felt free. She didn't have to abandon her roles. She simply started showing up in them from a place of honesty, not performance.

This is the power of realignment. You don't have to become someone new. You just need permission to return to who you've always been.

Sustainable Change: Creating Your Realignment Plan

Alignment isn't a destination—it's a practice. Here are three anchors to guide you:

1. **Start Where You Are**
   You don't need to have it all figured out. You just need to notice what's real and take one step toward it.

2. **Commit to Honesty**
   Your healing starts at the point of honesty. Begin with what's true—even if it's messy, even if it's painful. God can handle it.

3. **Return with Grace**
   You will drift from alignment. That doesn't mean you've failed. It means you're human. What matters is that you return—with grace, not guilt.

You don't have to keep pretending you're fine. You don't have to stay stuck in a life that no longer reflects your truth. And you absolutely do not need to be perfect to begin again.

You are not broken.
You are not too far gone.
You are becoming whole.

Let's keep going.

A Prayer for the Journey

God, I feel off.
I'm showing up, but I'm not fully present.
I miss the version of me who felt alive, connected, grounded in Your love.
Help me hear the truth beyond the noise.
Silence the critic in my mind and awaken the courage in my soul.
I'm not asking for a quick fix. I'm asking for wholeness.
Lead me back to myself. Lead me back to You.
Amen.

Chapter 2: The False Self You've Been Performing

"Who am I without the roles, the titles, or the mask?"

One of the greatest challenges I see in spiritual counseling is not that people don't know who they are—but that they've spent so much time becoming who they thought they had to be, they've forgotten how to be who they truly are.

We don't start out wearing masks. As children, we're beautifully raw—curious, expressive, honest about our needs, open about our emotions. But somewhere along the way, we start to learn what's expected. We pick up messages about who we should be in order to be safe, accepted, and loved.

We learn to adjust.
To perform.
To please.

We become adaptable, agreeable, responsible, impressive—whatever the moment calls for. And over time, those adjustments form a version of ourselves that feels polished on the outside but disconnected within.

This is what we call the **false self**—a self we've constructed in response to our environment, expectations, and experiences. Not because we're fake, but because we're *human*.

The Making of the False Self

The false self isn't evil. It's not a character flaw. It's a form of protection. When you were young, you may have needed to be the peacemaker in a chaotic home. Maybe you became the overachiever to win the approval of emotionally unavailable parents. Perhaps you learned to stay silent so you wouldn't be hurt. Or maybe you became "the strong one," always dependable, always resilient—even when you were breaking inside.

These patterns weren't random. They were *survival strategies*. You built them to navigate a world that felt too unpredictable or unsafe. And for a while, they worked.

But over time, what once protected you can start to confine you. You wake up one day and realize: *I've spent years becoming someone I'm not sure I want to be.*

When the Role Becomes a Prison

I remember a woman I counseled years ago—a brilliant leader and beloved by her community. To everyone else, she seemed vibrant and successful. But in our sessions, she kept repeating one phrase: *"I feel invisible."*

She had built her identity around being helpful, dependable, needed. She never said no. She met everyone else's needs while quietly ignoring her own. She wasn't lying about who she was—she just didn't know how to *stop performing* long enough to discover who she was beneath it all.

That's what the false self does. It keeps you busy managing an image, fulfilling a role, protecting a reputation. But all the while, your soul is starving for truth.

And here's the hard part: the world *rewards* the false self.

- It praises your productivity.
- It applauds your strength.
- It depends on your consistency.
- It celebrates your sacrifice.

But very few people stop to ask how *you're* doing. The applause becomes addictive. The role becomes familiar. And the longer you wear the mask, the harder it feels to take it off.

When You Start to Wonder, "Who Am I Without This?"

This is often where the spiritual unraveling begins. You've climbed the ladder, built the platform, checked all the boxes—and still, something feels off.

- You wonder who you are when no one needs you.
- You question your worth outside of your work.
- You struggle to feel loved without being "useful."
- You feel disconnected from your own heart, as if your soul is hidden beneath layers of expectation.

And maybe, just maybe, you've reached a point where you're tired of pretending. You're exhausted by the performance. You don't want to just be impressive anymore—you want to be *real*.

The Compassionate Naming

This chapter is not about shame. It's about compassion.

I want you to take a moment and consider the false self you've built. Not to judge it, but to understand it. What role did it play? What wound did it protect? What need was it trying to meet?

Maybe you became the perfectionist because you feared failure.
Maybe you became the caretaker because love felt conditional.
Maybe you became the achiever because you believed you had to earn your worth.

These false selves were formed in response to pain. But the presence of pain doesn't mean the absence of God. In fact, the opposite is true. God sees every mask we've worn, every performance we've rehearsed, and still gently calls us into truth.

> "Behold, you desire truth in the inward parts,
> And in the hidden part You will make me to know wisdom."
> *(Psalm 51:6)*

God doesn't want your performance—He wants *you*. The whole you. The real you. The you that existed before the world told you who you had to be.

Unmasking in God's Presence

The presence of God is the safest place to unmask.

You don't have to be perfect there. You don't have to impress Him. You don't have to pretend to be okay.

God sees beneath the layers, beyond the labels. He sees the child in you who still needs reassurance. He sees the leader in you who secretly longs to rest. He sees the servant in you who sometimes wishes to be served. And He calls all of it *beloved*.

You are not your titles. You are not your trauma. You are not your achievements.

You are a soul—created in the image of God, deeply loved, and called to live in truth.

The Sacred Work of Shedding

Letting go of the false self isn't a one-time event—it's a process. A sacred, often painful unraveling. You might find yourself mourning the parts of you that once made you feel safe. You may fear disappointing others. You may wonder what will be left when the performance ends.

But on the other side of that shedding is freedom.

You'll breathe deeper. You'll laugh more fully. You'll walk more lightly.

Because living from your true self is not just about *doing* less. It's about *being* more—more honest, more connected, more whole.

Questions for Realignment

In spiritual counseling, I often walk people through this simple but powerful set of questions:

1. What roles have you been playing out of obligation, not authenticity?

2. What expectations are you carrying that are no longer aligned with your soul?

3. Who are you when no one is looking, and no one is applauding?

4. What part of you have you silenced, hidden, or rejected in order to be accepted?

These questions aren't easy. But they're necessary if you want to live from the center of who you are instead of the surface of who you've become.

A Story from My Own Shedding

Years ago, I reached a breaking point in ministry. I was working tirelessly, constantly pouring out, always trying to "get it right." I had become the go-to person for everyone else's crises—but inside, I was unraveling.

I felt burned out, unseen, and unworthy. But instead of slowing down, I performed harder. I wore the mask of strength while silently falling apart. Until one day, someone I deeply respected told me I wasn't enough. That I had failed. And something inside me shattered.

That moment—though deeply painful—was also sacred. It forced me to confront the truth: I had built a false self to survive, but now it was time to *heal*. I didn't need to *be more*—I needed to *be real*. And that required me to stop performing and start surrendering.

Becoming Who You Truly Are

The false self is built on *who you think you need to be*.
The true self is rooted in *who God created you to be*.

Your true self isn't always the most confident or put-together version of you. Sometimes, it's the tender, messy, unsure parts of you that are finally safe enough to come forward. The true self is grounded, not grand. It doesn't strive to impress—it simply *is*.

You become your true self not by adding more to your life—but by removing what doesn't belong. The roles, the masks, the lies, the pressure. What's left is someone more familiar than you expected. Someone you've always been. Someone who finally feels like *you*.

How We Learn to Survive by Becoming Who We Think We Should Be

Some of us learned early that love had conditions. That it was safer to stay quiet, to shrink, to be helpful, or to shine only in ways that made others comfortable. We began shaping ourselves into the version of us that others expected.

And it worked. For a while.

But over time, those survival strategies became limitations. You kept showing up as the responsible one, the strong one, the fixer, the spiritual one—because it felt safer than letting people see the vulnerable, messy, human parts of you.

That false self helped you get through. But now it's keeping you from *living fully*.

Masks, Roles, and the Burden of Expectations

Here are a few masks I've seen people wear—not because they're inauthentic, but because they've forgotten they're allowed to take them off:

- **The Rescuer:** Always saving others, rarely asking for help
- **The Achiever:** Defined by productivity and performance
- **The Stoic:** Avoids vulnerability by staying emotionally distant
- **The Chameleon:** Adapts to every space, but loses their own identity
- **The Saint:** Performs spiritual strength while hiding their struggle

These roles are not your identity. They were tools for survival. And you are allowed to outgrow them.

The Spiritual Wound of Disconnection

The deeper cost of performing is *spiritual disconnection*—not because God has moved, but because we've covered our true selves with layers of expectation and shame. We show up in ministry, in marriage, in motherhood, in leadership—but we wonder why we feel numb or unseen.

This is the root of misalignment. When your spirit is saying one thing and your life is saying another, the soul feels divided. That division creates disconnection from self, from others, and from God.

But God doesn't bless the version of you you're pretending to be. He blesses the *real you*—the one He created, called, and sees beneath the performance.

Inner Exploration: Your Mask Inventory

Find a quiet space. Take a few deep breaths. With your journal open, reflect:

- What role do I most often play to feel safe or accepted?
- Where did I learn that I had to become that person?
- What would it feel like to let that mask go—even just for one day?

This isn't about abandoning responsibility. It's about reclaiming your authenticity.

Self-Assessment: False Self Check-In

Rank each of the following from 1 (Never) to 5 (Always):

1. I feel pressure to maintain a certain image or identity.
2. I often downplay my needs or emotions to avoid conflict.
3. I'm not sure who I am outside of my roles.

4. I struggle to rest unless I feel I've "earned" it.

5. I'm afraid others won't accept the real me.

6. I feel emotionally exhausted by the version of myself I present.

Results & Reflection:

- **Mostly 1–2s:** You're beginning to live authentically—keep nurturing that space.

- **Mostly 3s:** You're in the middle of your unmasking—stay curious and gentle.

- **Mostly 4–5s:** You're likely over-identifying with a false self—begin creating safe places for truth to emerge.

Practical Application: Daily Unmasking Practice

Try this gentle practice to begin releasing what no longer fits:

"I Am Not My Role" Mantra

Each morning, stand in front of a mirror. Place your hand over your heart and say:
I am not what I do. I am not what I fix. I am not what others expect. I am who God created me to be—loved, seen, chosen, and whole.

Repeat it until your body begins to believe it.

Weekly Practice: Real Talk with Someone Safe

Choose one person this week and share something you've been carrying behind the mask. Maybe it's fear, fatigue, or a hidden dream. Allow yourself to be seen—not as "the strong one," but as the whole you.

Notice what it feels like to tell the truth and still be loved.

Mind-Body-Spirit Practice: Embodied Prayer for Truth

When you feel disconnected, try this grounding prayer:

1. Sit or stand with feet flat on the floor.

2. Place your hands open on your lap.

3. Breathe deeply and slowly repeat:

    - *"I release who I had to be..."*

    - *"I receive who I'm becoming..."*

    - *"God, anchor me in truth."*

Let your body learn what alignment feels like.

Emotional Resilience: Moving Through the Fear of Being Seen

Unmasking can feel risky. Vulnerability often brings fear. But hiding has its own cost—disconnection, exhaustion, and shame.

When fear rises, remember:

- Your truth does not make you a burden.

- Your needs do not make you weak.

- The real you is worthy of love and belonging.

The people meant for your journey will celebrate your becoming, not punish your authenticity.

Terrence's Return

Terrence was a gifted leader, beloved in his career and community—but behind closed doors, he was unraveling. "I've spent years being who people needed me to be," he confessed. "And I don't even know who I am anymore."

Through guided journaling, soul care practices, and safe spaces for vulnerability, Terrence began peeling back the layers. He didn't lose himself—he *found* himself. He returned to music. He rediscovered joy. He stopped overfunctioning. "I'm no longer living to be liked," he said. "I'm living to be whole."

Sustainable Change: A Life Without the Mask

You won't become your true self in a day. But you can choose honesty every day—and those choices will create a life of alignment.

Start Here:

- **Build Safe Circles:** Identify 1–2 people where you can be fully yourself. Let them witness you.

- **Revisit Your Roles:** Monthly, ask: *Which roles are life-giving? Which are masking my truth?*

- **Stay Flexible:** You are allowed to grow. Who you are today may not be who you need to be tomorrow.

Community Reflection: #UnmaskOneThing

Share one role, label, or expectation you're letting go of this week. Use the hashtag **#UnmaskOneThing** to inspire others and be inspired by those also choosing authenticity over appearance.

God doesn't need the version of you who's always strong, always smiling, always "on." He wants *you*. Fully human. Fully seen. Fully loved. It's time to stop performing for the worth you already have.

You are not your mask.
You are not your role.
You are already whole.

Let's keep uncovering the truth.

Reflection Questions

1. What false roles or expectations have you adopted in your life?

2. How have those roles helped you survive? In what ways are they now holding you back?

3. What does your true self long to express or reclaim?

4. Who in your life supports the real you—not just the version you perform?

5. What would it feel like to live one day without the mask?

Let this chapter be your invitation—not to abandon who you've been, but to embrace who you truly are. The false self helped you survive, but you're not here to survive anymore.

You're here to live—whole, free, and fully aligned with who God created you to be.

A Prayer for Shedding the False Self

God, I've spent so much time becoming who I thought I had to be.
I've worn the mask, played the role, chased the applause.
But I'm tired of pretending.
I want to come home to myself.
Help me name the false self without shame.
Help me shed the pressure without fear.
Show me the truth of who You created me to be.
I'm ready to live from the inside out.
Amen.

Chapter 3: Why Fixes Haven't Worked

"You've tried everything—except facing what's underneath."

If I had a dollar for every time someone sat across from me in a spiritual counseling session and said, *"I've tried everything, and I still feel stuck"*, I could fund a retreat for every soul craving breakthrough.

They say things like:

- "I read all the devotionals."

- "I wrote the vision board."

- "I journal every morning."

- "I've gone to therapy."

- "I speak the affirmations."

- "I've fasted. I've prayed. I've done the work."

And yet, they still feel heavy. Still feel anxious. Still repeat the same relational patterns. Still numb with distraction, overcommitment, or endless scrolling. Still wonder, *Why don't I feel free—even though I'm doing all the right things?*

If this sounds like you, hear me when I say: **your frustration is valid. Your exhaustion is real. And your efforts are not wasted.**

But here's what I've learned—not just as a clinical chaplain, but as someone who's lived it:

> **Most of us have been given tools that treat our symptoms—not our soul.**

You're Not Lazy—You're Undernourished

The problem isn't that you're undisciplined or spiritually lazy. The problem is that you've been operating from depletion for far too long. You've tried to *fix* what actually needs to be *felt*. You've tried to *achieve* what actually needs to be *healed*. And you've tried to *change* from the outside in—without addressing what's actually happening within.

Let's be honest: it's easier to download another podcast than to sit in silence with your grief. It's easier to try a new goal-setting app than to confront your unspoken shame. It's easier to highlight your Bible than to face the parts of your story you'd rather forget.

But transformation doesn't happen through hustle. It happens through *honesty*.

And that kind of truth-telling takes courage.

The Illusion of the "Quick Fix"

We live in a world that loves the illusion of instant change. We want three steps, a morning routine, or a perfectly curated affirmation list. We want to *feel better* without having to *become different*.

But the truth is, there is no quick fix for the soul. Because the soul is sacred. And sacred things require sacred attention.

Let me say this clearly: **you don't need another fix—you need a foundation.**

That foundation is built, not on effort alone, but on *alignment*. Alignment with your truth. Alignment with your core values. Alignment with God's love. And alignment only happens when you slow down long enough to face what's *underneath* the surface.

What Surface Fixes Can't Touch

Here's what devotionals, planners, or positive quotes can't always touch:

- **The childhood wound** you never processed.

- **The betrayal** you forgave outwardly but never grieved inwardly.

- **The internalized shame** you carry like a secret weight.

- **The identity confusion** that has you hustling for worth.

- **The unspoken sadness** that leaks out in anger or withdrawal.

- **The inner critic** that sounds like a parent, a pastor, or an ex.

You can't organize your way out of emotional pain. You can't schedule your way out of spiritual disconnection. You can't perform your way into peace.

You can't heal what you never name.
And you can't change if you only address the *symptom*, not the *source*.

The Trap of Performing Healing

One of the most common blocks to deep healing is *performing healing*—trying to look the part without doing the inner work. You light the candle, play the worship music, write the gratitude list—and all of that is good. But if you're still afraid to be *alone with your truth*, none of it will root.

It's not about looking healed.
It's about *becoming whole*.

And wholeness means facing the parts of you you've pushed aside—the anger, the disappointment, the fear, the unmet needs. It means telling the truth about your life, not just repeating spiritual clichés.

God is not afraid of your mess.
He's not shocked by your struggle.
He doesn't need you to get it all together.
He just wants your *honesty*.

What If It's Not Working Because It's Not Deep Enough?

If the tools you've been using aren't working, it doesn't mean you've failed—it may simply mean the tools were never meant to reach the *depth* you needed.

You can't bandage a broken bone with a Bible verse. Scripture is powerful. But even Scripture tells us to "guard our heart" and "renew our mind." That implies *depth work*. Not a quick patch, but a deep reworking of our inner life.

God doesn't bypass your humanity to transform your spirit. He heals both. But that healing starts by going beneath the surface.

The Invitation to Go Deeper

The people I've walked with in hospice, recovery, grief counseling, and spiritual care all have one thing in common: at some point, they stopped reaching outward and started turning inward. They began asking deeper questions.

Not "What should I do next?"
But, "What am I *really* feeling?"
Not "How do I fix this?"
But, "What is this pain trying to teach me?"
Not "How do I get back to normal?"
But, "What kind of life do I want to build from here?"

Those are the questions that change us. Not because they offer fast answers—but because they call us back to alignment.

How the Soul Speaks

The soul doesn't speak in bullet points or to-do lists. It speaks in longings. In aches. In tears that surprise you. In restlessness you can't explain. In fatigue that no amount of sleep seems to fix.

And too often, we misinterpret those signals.

- We call the anxiety "a lack of faith," when it might be a trauma response.

- We call the sadness "laziness," when it might be ungrieved loss.

- We call the burnout "a sign to push harder," when it might be your soul saying, *"Please slow down."*

The soul is always speaking. The question is: are you listening?

The Gift of Hitting a Wall

As painful as it is, hitting a wall can be a gift. When nothing works, and you're too tired to keep pretending, you finally become available for *truth*. You stop trying to manipulate healing and start surrendering to it.

You stop saying:

- "What's wrong with me?"
  And start asking:

- "What have I been avoiding?"

- "What parts of me need compassion, not correction?"

- "What would it look like to move through this with God, not just for Him?"

That's when the work deepens. That's when healing begins.

From Coping to Healing

Coping mechanisms aren't bad—they're just incomplete. They help you survive. But you weren't created just to survive. You were created to *live*.

That means moving beyond:

- **Distraction** → to **intention**

- **Overworking** → to **inner stillness**

- **Avoidance** → to **acceptance**

- **Perfectionism** → to **presence**

God doesn't want you to live on spiritual autopilot. He wants you to *thrive in awareness*—to know who you are, what you feel, what you need, and where He is in the midst of it.

Real Healing Requires Inner Alignment

True healing starts when your spirit, soul, and body come into alignment.

- Your **spirit** reconnects with God's truth.

- Your **soul** (your mind, will, and emotions) gets honest, feels deeply, and receives care.

- Your **body** releases stored stress, trauma, and tension through movement, rest, and nourishment.

Most people only engage in one or two of these areas. But when all three align, you don't just feel better—you *become whole.*

This is the kind of healing that doesn't just change your behavior. It changes your *being.*

A Better Way: From Surface to Soul

Instead of fixing your life externally, this chapter invites you to:

- *Name what's underneath your patterns.*

- *Stop outsourcing your peace to productivity.*

- *Bring your full self—your honest, hurting, healing self—to God.*

- *Replace performance with presence.*

Because true peace isn't found in control. It's found in *connection*—to yourself and to God.

You're Not Too Far Gone

If you've been feeling like healing isn't working for you—if you've tried everything and still feel stuck—I want you to know:

You are not too far gone.
You are not beyond repair.
You are not failing at faith.

You're just being invited to go deeper.

The Limits of Productivity, Pop Psychology, and Positive Thinking

We live in a culture obsessed with fast answers and surface upgrades. Productivity tells you to do more. Pop psychology tells you to change your mindset. Positive thinking tells you to just stay grateful. But when your soul is aching, these "solutions" can feel like spiritual bypassing.

Here's what often happens:

- **Productivity** becomes another form of escape. You stay busy to avoid feeling.

- **Pop psychology** offers insight without embodiment. You know what's wrong, but still feel stuck.

- **Positive thinking** pressures you to suppress real emotion in favor of performance.

These things are not bad. In fact, they can be helpful when integrated *with* deeper healing. But on their own, they often reinforce the belief that you should be able to "fix" yourself with more effort.

But wholeness is not effort—it's embodiment.
And healing doesn't come through hustling—it comes through honesty.

Why Information Alone Doesn't Transform

You can know all the right things and still feel misaligned. You can read Scripture, quote affirmations, attend every church service—and still feel numb, anxious, or unfulfilled. Why? Because information alone doesn't change people. **Integration does.**

Here's what integration means:

- Your beliefs are reflected in your behaviors.
- Your truth is felt in your body, not just your head.
- Your relationship with God isn't just theoretical—it's transformative.
- Your values shape your schedule, not the other way around.

Transformation happens when your soul, mind, body, and spirit begin moving in the same direction. That's where alignment becomes real.

Inner Exploration: What's Really Going On?

Create a quiet space and ask yourself:

- What have I tried to feel better—and why hasn't it worked?
- Have I been focused on *managing symptoms* instead of *healing roots*?
- What part of me is asking to be seen, heard, or healed—not fixed?

Let your answers flow honestly. This is not about judgment. This is about uncovering what's true.

Self-Assessment: Quick Fix vs. Deep Work

Rate the following statements from 1 (Never) to 5 (Always):

1. I constantly seek new strategies or content to solve my emotional unrest.

2. I feel like I'm always "doing the work," but still don't feel different.

3. I find it difficult to sit in silence without needing to fix or plan.

4. I use spiritual language to avoid difficult emotions.

5. I feel overwhelmed by how much I "know" without knowing how to apply it.

Scoring:

- **5–10:** You're in a good place to begin deeper integration.

- **11–18:** You're aware, but may be caught in cycles of information overload.

- **19–25:** It's time to simplify and embody your truth—less content, more connection.

The Missing Ingredient: Integration and Inner Connection

Most of what's marketed as transformation is really just repackaged performance. But true, sustainable change happens through integration—when your head, heart, habits, and spirit begin to operate in agreement.

Here's what integration looks like:

- You don't just know God's peace—you embody it at your pace.
- You don't just understand boundaries—you set and honor them.
- You don't just talk about rest—you actually practice it.
- You don't just recognize trauma—you give space to process and heal it.

Integration isn't flashy. It's faithful. It's often slow. But it's where real wholeness is born.

Practical Application: Begin Integrating Now

You don't need to do more. You need to *practice presence* in small, intentional ways.

Daily Practice: Feel – Name – Align

1. **Feel** – Pause. What do I feel right now—emotionally, physically, spiritually?

2. **Name** – What is the feeling connected to? What's the deeper message?

3. **Align** – What is one action or mindset that brings me closer to truth?

Example:
Feeling: Anxious
Naming: I'm afraid I'll disappoint others if I say no
Aligning: I say no anyway, trusting that peace matters more than performance

---

Spiritual Care Practice: Weekly "One-Thing" Reset

Each week, reflect:

- What's *one thing* I'm learning?

- How can I *live* that truth this week?

Resist the urge to do more. Let one truth guide your week. Let it sink into your schedule, your decisions, your breath.

Mind-Body-Spirit Practice: Grounded Presence Prayer

1. Sit quietly.

2. Inhale for 4 counts: *"God is with me."*

3. Exhale for 6 counts: *"And I am safe."*

4. Repeat slowly for 2–5 minutes.

5. Ask: *What truth do I need to embody today?*

Let your body begin to feel the truth your spirit already knows.

Emotional Resilience: When Progress Feels Invisible

Sometimes we expect healing to feel dramatic. But integration often feels like peace where there used to be panic. Rest where there used to be striving. Gentleness where there used to be shame.

Signs that you're integrating:

- You notice when you're misaligned—without judgment.
- You pause before reacting.
- You speak to yourself more kindly.
- You don't abandon yourself in order to be liked.

That's real, embodied progress

Nicole's Turning Point

Nicole had read every book on spiritual growth. She knew the language. She had all the tools. But she still felt emotionally disconnected. "I've consumed so much," she told me. "But I'm not changing."

We simplified everything. One breath prayer in the morning. One aligned "yes" each day. One truth journal entry at night. Within weeks, her anxiety lessened. Her clarity returned. "I stopped trying to fix myself," she said. "And started trusting myself. And God."

That's integration.

Sustainable Change: From Insight to Embodiment

Lasting change doesn't come from knowing more. It comes from living what you already know.

Integration Plan:

- Choose one aligned practice to repeat daily (breath prayer, body scan, truth journaling)

- Block 15 minutes each week for stillness and self-reflection

- Invite God to speak—not to correct you, but to *center* you

- Revisit what's *working*, and adjust what's not—without shame

Community Engagement: #LiveItNotLearnIt

This week, choose one truth to embody—not just read or post about. Share what it looks like to *live it* using the hashtag **#LiveItNotLearnIt**. Let others walk with you on the path of integration.

You don't need more content.
You need more connection.
You don't need more knowledge.
You need more embodiment.
You don't need to be fixed.
You need to *feel*—and trust that healing will follow.

You are already becoming whole. One aligned moment at a time.

Reflection Questions

1. What surface-level "fixes" have you been relying on that no longer feel effective?

2. What emotional patterns or struggles keep resurfacing in your life?

3. What part of your story, pain, or identity might need deeper attention?

4. What would it look like to move from performance to presence in your healing journey?

5. What small step can you take this week to connect with your soul—not just your schedule?

The truth is, you're not doing it wrong. You're just being invited to stop *fixing* and start *feeling*. To stop *striving* and start *surrendering*. To stop living on the surface—and come home to your soul.

A Prayer for Deeper Healing

God, I'm tired of trying to fix myself.
I've done the steps, read the books, made the lists.
But I still feel stuck. Still feel weary. Still feel unsure.
I don't want another surface solution. I want real healing.
Help me slow down and listen to what my soul is trying to say.
Show me what's underneath my patterns.
Teach me how to walk with You into the deeper places.
I trust that You don't just want me to function.
You want me to flourish.
And You're willing to meet me in the root of my pain, not just the fruit.
Amen.

Section 2: Returning to Center – The Work of Reconnection

Chapter 4: Your Inner Compass – Values, Voice & Vision

"God's direction for your life is already within you—it just needs space to speak."

When life feels misaligned, it's rarely because we lack effort. Most of us are *trying*. We're showing up. We're working hard. We're following the rules and carrying the load. But even in all of that effort, we can feel off-center—adrift, unclear, or quietly dissatisfied.

You may be doing everything "right" by the world's standards. And yet, you're still asking:

- *Why does my life feel disconnected from who I really am?*

- *Why do I feel so busy, but so unfulfilled?*

- *Why can I hear everyone else's voice so clearly, but not my own?*

These questions aren't signs of weakness. They're sacred invitations to return to your **inner compass**—that deep, God-planted sense of direction that is anchored in truth, guided by grace, and aligned with your purpose.

The Inner Compass You've Been Carrying All Along

You were not created to live a life of confusion or chaos. You were created with clarity. The God who formed your soul also embedded within you a compass—a set of spiritual and emotional guideposts designed to lead you back to yourself and back to Him.

This compass is made up of three key elements:

1. **Values** – What matters most to you.

2. **Voice** – Your unique perspective, intuition, and spiritual discernment.

3. **Vision** – The God-given picture of the life you are meant to live.

When these are clear and honored, your life flows with meaning and peace. When they're ignored, silenced, or overridden by pressure, your soul starts to rebel.

> *"You will hear a voice behind you, saying, 'This is the way; walk in it.'"*
> *(Isaiah 30:21)*

The voice is already there. The guidance already exists. But often, we've filled our lives with so much *noise*—expectations, distractions, performance—that we can't hear the still, sacred voice that's trying to guide us from within.

Disconnection from the Compass

As a chaplain, I've sat with people from every walk of life—pastors, counselors, business owners, single moms or dads, retirees—who found themselves at a crossroads. They had spent years building lives that looked successful on the outside, but internally, something was missing.

- A gifted leader who felt numb in their calling.
- A faithful parent who felt invisible in their own home.
- A burnt-out minister who hadn't heard God's voice in months.

What they all had in common wasn't a lack of ability. It was a loss of *alignment.* They were so busy fulfilling roles that they forgot to check in with their own soul. Their inner compass was still present—it had just been buried beneath the clutter of performance, people-pleasing, and pressure.

You don't need a new title or a new assignment. You need to **rediscover who you are beneath what you do.**

Rediscovering Your Values

Values are the principles and truths that matter most to your soul. They are non-negotiable. They are rooted in who you are, not just what you've been taught. And when you live in alignment with them, life feels grounded—even when it's hard.

Here's the challenge: most people have never taken the time to define their values for themselves. Instead, they inherit them.

- From their parents.
- From their church.

- From their culture.
- From social media.
- From survival.

And while those influences may have shaped you, they don't always reflect the *truest* parts of you.

To reconnect with your values, ask yourself:

- When do I feel most alive?
- What am I unwilling to compromise, even when it's hard?
- When have I felt most disconnected from myself, and what was missing?

Maybe you value authenticity, but you've been playing it safe to fit in.
Maybe you value rest, but you've been stuck in hustle culture.
Maybe you value intimacy with God, but you've been too busy serving to actually sit in His presence.

These misalignments aren't moral failings. They're indicators. And they are inviting you back to the truth.

Reclaiming Your Voice

So many people I counsel tell me they've lost their voice—not literally, but spiritually. They've become so conditioned to meet the expectations of others that they no longer trust their own inner knowing.

But here's what I want you to remember: **your voice is sacred. Your discernment is divine. Your intuition is a gift.**

God speaks not only through thunder and lightning, but through *whispers*, *nudges*, and *gut feelings*. When you override your own voice for too long, you lose your sense of internal safety. You start looking for validation in people, programs, or productivity instead of listening inward.

I'm not talking about selfishness or rebellion—I'm talking about the quiet courage to say:

- "This doesn't feel right."

- "God is leading me in a different direction."

- "I don't have peace about this."

- "I need space to hear clearly."

You don't have to explain your soul's journey to everyone. But you do have to *honor it*.

> "My sheep hear My voice, and I know them, and they follow Me."
> (John 10:27)

If you are His, then His voice is not far from you—it's within you. It may be buried under noise, trauma, or fear, but it is *not lost*.

Seeing Your Vision Again

Somewhere in your life, God gave you a **vision**—a glimpse of what could be. A sense of purpose that stirred your heart. A dream, a calling, a burden that lit a fire in your soul.

But over time, that vision may have faded. Life got loud. Responsibilities piled up. Detours and delays discouraged you. And now, when you try to access that dream, it feels distant—like someone else's life.

I want to tell you something that I tell people in spiritual care all the time:

If the vision still lives in you, it's not too late.

God doesn't give us dreams as teasers. He gives them as *invitations*. Even if your path looks different than you expected—even if it's taken longer than you thought—your vision is still valid. You may just need to look at it through a new lens.

Sometimes your vision evolves as *you* evolve. That's okay. Vision is not always about a career or a platform. Sometimes it's about the kind of life you want to live, the kind of person you want to become, the legacy you want to leave behind.

To reconnect with your vision, ask:

- What desires has God placed on my heart that won't go away?
- What injustices or issues stir me to action or tears?
- What brings me deep joy—not just momentary happiness?
- What kind of life feels like *peace* to me?

The answers may not come all at once. But if you create space for stillness, the vision will begin to reappear—one layer at a time.

When You Live Out of Alignment

When your values, voice, and vision are disconnected, you'll know. Your body will feel it. Your emotions will echo it. Your spirit will grieve it.

You'll feel:

- Restless, even when life is full.

- Irritable, even when no one has done anything wrong.

- Spiritually distant, even when you're going through the motions.

These are symptoms of misalignment. They aren't punishments—they're prompts. Signals from your soul that say: *This isn't working. Come back to the center.*

Giving Yourself Permission to Realign

Realignment doesn't require you to blow up your life or abandon your responsibilities. It simply requires *permission*—to pause, to listen, to re-center.

That may mean:

- Saying "no" to something you've outgrown.

- Choosing rest over another meeting.

- Making space for prayer, reflection, or journaling.

- Asking for help instead of pushing through alone.

You don't have to rush back into clarity. Just start by being *present* with what your soul is trying to say.

God Leads from the Inside Out

In the Old Testament, God led His people with pillars of fire and cloud. Today, He often leads through inner peace, conviction, and clarity. We are no longer following signs in the sky—we are following the *Spirit within*.

> *"The Spirit Himself bears witness with our spirit that we are children of God."*
> *(Romans 8:16)*

That same Spirit speaks through your values, your voice, and your vision. You don't have to chase signs when you're already carrying the source. You just need space to listen, space to trust, space to remember.

Rediscovering What Actually Matters to You

It's easy to lose sight of what matters when life moves fast. We say "yes" to things we don't love, tolerate relationships that drain us, and pursue goals that don't fulfill us—all because we've forgotten what we truly value.

Rediscovering your values doesn't mean rejecting everything. It means *realigning* with what God has placed within you as sacred and non-negotiable.

When you live in alignment with your values:

- Your decisions become clearer
- Your relationships become more honest
- Your time and energy feel more purposeful
- Your life starts to reflect your *soul*, not just your schedule

---

Inner Exploration: Reconnecting to the Voice Within

Set aside 10–15 quiet minutes. Light a candle. Sit still. Ask:

- What do I long for in this season—really?
- What would I choose if I wasn't afraid of disappointing anyone?
- What did I love doing before I felt pressure to be productive?

Let the answers rise without editing them. This is your soul speaking.

Self-Assessment: Core Values Clarifier

Rate the following values from 1 (Not Important) to 5 (Deeply Important):

- Integrity
- Compassion
- Creativity

- Spirituality
- Justice
- Freedom
- Rest
- Growth
- Service
- Simplicity
- Authenticity
- Family
- Truth
- Peace
- Joy

Reflection Questions:

- Which 3–5 values feel *non-negotiable* right now?
- Are these values visible in your current life?
- What needs to shift to honor these values more fully?

Tailored Strategies: Start Where You Are

Now that you've identified your top values, choose one to *honor intentionally* this week.

If you value...

- **Peace:** Protect time for stillness. Say no without over-explaining.

- **Creativity:** Block time to create without needing it to be "useful."

- **Spirituality:** Carve out daily space to connect with God—not for performance, but for presence.

- **Family:** Be fully present with a loved one—no phone, no multitasking.

- **Rest:** Cancel or postpone something that's draining you. Choose replenishment.

The smallest shifts often lead to the deepest change.

Reclaiming the Voice Underneath the Noise

When you've spent years performing, pleasing, or producing, your voice can become buried beneath the noise of others' expectations. But it's still there—quiet, steady, sacred.

That voice is:

- The nudge that says *"this doesn't feel right"*
- The whisper that says *"there's more for you"*
- The longing that says *"you were made for peace, not pressure"*

Reclaiming your voice is a spiritual act. It's giving yourself permission to *listen*, trust, and follow the God-breathed wisdom already within you.

Practical Application: Daily Compass Check-In

Each morning or evening, ask:

- *Did I live in alignment with my values today?*
- *Where did I ignore or abandon my voice?*
- *What will I do differently tomorrow to honor who I am?*

Let these questions become a rhythm—not to judge yourself, but to realign gently and consistently.

Mind-Body-Spirit Practice: Centering Breath & Prayer

Try this 3-minute practice when you feel scattered or unclear:

1. Sit comfortably. Feet grounded.

2. Inhale deeply: *"God, anchor me in truth."*

3. Exhale slowly: *"Let me hear my own voice again."*

4. Place your hand on your heart and ask: *What matters most today?*

Let your body register that alignment is safe, not rushed.

Emotional Resilience: When Clarity Feels Risky

Sometimes, rediscovering your values will require uncomfortable shifts. You may disappoint others. You may let go of long-standing commitments. You may question old goals. That's not rebellion—it's *realignment*.

You're not betraying others by becoming more of yourself.
You're just choosing *truth over performance*, peace over pressure.

God will not leave you when you live from your truth. He will *lead* you in it.

Jasmine's Voice

Jasmine, a nonprofit founder, came into spiritual care feeling suffocated by expectations. "I don't even know what *I* want anymore," she said. Through soul reflection and values work, she realized that **presence**—with herself, her family, and God—was her deepest value. She began setting new boundaries and redesigning her schedule around that truth. "I found my voice again," she told me. "And it didn't sound like obligation—it sounded like joy."

Sustainable Change: A Compass You Can Carry

Your values are your compass. They are how you return to center when life gets noisy.

Monthly Compass Review:

- What's changed this season?
- Which value needs more attention?
- Where am I drifting—and how can I return?

Create a "Yes Filter": Before committing to anything, ask:
Does this reflect my top values? Will it bring me closer to peace or pull me away from it?

Community Engagement: #VoiceAndValues

Share your top 3 values and one way you're honoring your voice this week. Use the hashtag **#VoiceAndValues** to inspire others and reflect on the beauty of becoming who you really are.

You already have a compass within you. You don't need to search for purpose in performance. You don't need to be loud to be clear. Your values are valid. Your voice is sacred. Your vision is unfolding.

You don't have to become someone else to feel whole.
You only need to *return to who you are*.

Let's keep going.

Reflection Questions

1. What values do you hold most sacred—and are they reflected in how you live?

2. In what areas of life have you silenced your own voice?

3. What longings, dreams, or visions has God placed on your heart that you've neglected?

4. Where do you feel out of alignment in your life?

5. What's one small shift you can make this week to reconnect with your inner compass?

You don't have to live on autopilot. You don't have to keep chasing a version of life that isn't rooted in who you are. God is calling you—not just to be busy or impressive—but to be *whole*.

The answers you seek are already within. The compass hasn't been lost. It's just waiting for space to speak.

A Prayer to Reconnect With Your Inner Compass

God, I've been living disconnected—
from my truth, from my heart, from my direction.
I've been too busy performing to pause.
Too consumed with doing to remember who I am.

I want to come back to center.
Back to the values that matter.
Back to the voice You gave me.
Back to the vision that still burns quietly within me.

Speak, Lord. Even in the silence.
Remind me that Your direction is not far—
It's within me.
And I am safe to listen.
Amen.

Chapter 5: Healing What's Hidden

"You cannot heal what you won't name. And you cannot name what you're afraid to feel."

Let's start with a truth that's more common than we admit:

We aren't just overwhelmed by busy schedules.
We're overwhelmed by *buried pain*.
We're not just misaligned in habits.
We're misaligned because of *hidden wounds*.

And here's the most tender part:
Underneath that misalignment is not always rebellion. It's not laziness or avoidance.
More often—it's *grief*. It's *fear*. It's *exhaustion*.
It's pain that's been waiting to be heard.

We've learned to hide it well. We smile. We serve. We perform.
We spiritualize our pain because that feels safer than facing it.
But the ache doesn't leave just because we've labeled it with Christian language.
We may say things like:

- "God's in control," when what we really feel is *powerless*.

- "I'm too blessed to be stressed," when what we really feel is *burdened*.

- "I'm fine," when we're actually falling apart on the inside.

You're not alone in this.

Pain in Disguise

Pain is clever. It doesn't always show up the way we expect.

Sometimes it hides behind:

- **High-functioning behaviors** – you stay busy so you don't have to feel.

- **Perfectionism** – you control the external because your internal world feels chaotic.

- **Caretaking** – you pour into others because you don't know how to pour into yourself.

- **Hyper-spirituality** – you use spiritual language to bypass emotional honesty.

These aren't flaws. They're responses. They're ways your nervous system has learned to cope. But coping is not the same as *healing*.

Healing requires presence. Healing requires honesty. Healing requires space for what's hidden to come to light.

You Are Not Broken—You Are Bruised

I've sat with people who felt ashamed of their pain because they thought healing should've happened by now. They'd ask:

- "Why am I still struggling with this?"
- "Why do I shut down every time someone gets close?"
- "Why can't I just move on?"

My response is always the same:
You are not broken. You are bruised.
And bruises—when tended to with *truth and tenderness*—heal.

We don't shame bruises. We don't rush them. We *witness* them. We pay attention to what they're telling us. We invite God into the places we've tried to protect.

> *"The Lord is near to the brokenhearted and saves the crushed in spirit."*
> *(Psalm 34:18)*

God doesn't bypass your pain. He *enters it*. And He invites you to do the same.

Naming What Hurts

One of the most important steps in healing is the courage to *name* what you've been avoiding. You can't change what you're not willing to face. You can't release what you're not willing to feel.

But I want you to know: facing your pain is not the same as being consumed by it. Naming it doesn't mean you're giving it power. It means you're finally giving it *presence*.

Some questions to help you start:

- What have I been avoiding feeling?

- What emotions do I judge as "too much" or "too weak"?

- What memories still trigger me, even if I pretend they don't?

- What parts of my story still feel unhealed or unfinished?

You don't need to have all the answers. Just the *willingness* to look.

The Body Keeps the Score—and the Soul Holds the Story

Pain isn't just emotional—it's embodied.
If you've ever felt tension in your shoulders during stress, tightness in your chest during grief, or a pit in your stomach during conflict, you know this is true.

Your body stores what your mouth doesn't speak. Your muscles remember what your mind tried to forget. And your soul holds the stories you were too afraid to tell.

That's why true healing must be holistic—it must involve your spirit, soul, and body. You can't just talk your way out of pain. You have to feel your way *through* it—with God as your guide.

Healing doesn't always happen in grand moments.
Sometimes it looks like:

- Crying for the first time in months.

- Finally saying out loud what happened to you.

- Admitting that you're angry with God—and staying in the conversation.

- Realizing that numbness was never peace—it was protection.

The Mask of Strength

Many of us have worn the mask of strength for so long that we forgot how to be soft.
We learned early that vulnerability was risky. That crying was weakness. That needing help made us a burden.

So we became strong. We became reliable. We became the one who holds it all together.

But the mask of strength becomes a prison when it keeps you from healing.

Sometimes the strongest thing you can do is fall apart. Sometimes the holiest thing you can do is *feel*. Sometimes the most spiritual thing you can do is *rest*.

Your softness is not your weakness. It's where healing begins.

Avoidance Is Not the Same as Healing

You can't heal what you refuse to feel.
And you can't release what you never fully acknowledged.

Avoidance might protect you temporarily, but it also keeps you in bondage. It may sound like:

- "That was a long time ago—I'm over it."

- "It wasn't that bad. Other people have it worse."

- "I just need to stay busy and keep going."

But your soul knows better.
The ache beneath the surface. The sudden tearfulness. The anxiety that won't go away.
These are not signs of failure. They're invitations to *go deeper*.

God's Tenderness Is Safe for Your Wounds

One of the most beautiful truths I've learned in spiritual care is this:
God can handle what you've been hiding.

He is not scared of your trauma. He is not shocked by your anger. He is not disappointed in your sorrow.

Where others may have told you to "get over it," God invites you to *walk through it*—with Him beside you every step of the way.

> "He heals the brokenhearted and binds up their wounds."
> (Psalm 147:3)

God doesn't rush you. He doesn't shame you. He doesn't use your pain as punishment.

He enters your wounds like a skilled surgeon—precise, patient, and purposeful.

Witnessing Before Fixing

We often rush to fix what God first wants us to *feel*.
We want resolution, but God offers *revelation*.
Not for the sake of re-traumatizing us—but for the sake of *freeing* us.

Healing is not about rehashing everything that ever hurt you.
It's about finally telling the truth to yourself—without judgment.

When we witness our pain with compassion, we make room for God's comfort.

You might say:

- "That hurt more than I admitted at the time."

- "I never got to grieve that loss."

- "I was made to feel like I had to be okay before I really was."

And God responds, "I know. And I was there. And I'm here now."

The Slow Work of Restoration

There is no fast track to wholeness.
There is only the *faithful, slow work* of restoration.

Healing is often quiet.
It happens in small, sacred shifts:

- One honest conversation.

- One deep breath.

- One journal entry that finally tells the truth.

- One moment where you *don't* override your own needs.

You may not feel "healed" overnight.
But day by day, truth by truth, you are returning to yourself.

From Hidden to Held

What's been hidden can finally be *held*—not with fear, but with love.

The parts of you that feel too complicated?
God calls them worthy.

The feelings that feel too messy?
God calls them sacred.

The pain that feels too heavy?
God doesn't demand you carry it alone.

He is the One who carries what we can't.
The One who comforts what we can't explain.
The One who heals what we've hidden for far too long.

Naming and Nurturing the Unhealed Parts of You

For many of us, the deepest parts of our pain have never been named—only managed. Maybe you were taught to "be strong," "stay grateful," or "just have faith." So you put on a smile, got back to work, and buried the ache. But healing doesn't happen through avoidance. It happens through awareness. Through invitation. Through compassion.

To nurture what's unhealed, you must begin by seeing it. Without judgment. Without fixing. With kindness.

These parts of you don't need to be shamed. They need to be acknowledged, comforted, and slowly reintegrated into your story—not as liabilities, but as invitations to deeper wholeness.

Inner Exploration: The Unseen Wounds

Create sacred space for reflection. Light a candle. Sit in stillness. Ask:

- What part of me feels unseen, unspoken, or silenced?
- What pain have I minimized, spiritualized, or denied?
- What would it feel like to let this part of me be seen with compassion?

Let this be a space of presence, not pressure. You don't need to solve anything—you just need to listen.

Self-Assessment: Hidden Wounds Inventory

Rate each statement from 1 (Rarely) to 5 (Often):

1. I feel emotionally disconnected or numb.

2. I struggle to name or express my true feelings.

3. I avoid silence or stillness because it brings up discomfort.

4. I carry shame about parts of my past or personality.

5. I use spiritual practices to avoid emotional honesty.

6. I often feel the need to be strong, even when I'm hurting.

Results:

- **5–10:** You're creating space for healing. Keep tending gently.

- **11–18:** Your wounds are asking for attention—approach them slowly and with grace.

- **19–30:** Deep pain is present. Consider engaging in deeper soul work, therapy, or guided spiritual care.

How Trauma, Shame, and Spiritual Wounds Hijack Alignment

These three forces are often at the root of our disconnection:

- **Trauma** teaches your body that the world isn't safe.

- **Shame** convinces you that *you* are the problem.

- **Spiritual wounding** tells you God only accepts the polished, perfect parts of you.

When these remain hidden, they shape our decisions, our boundaries, our relationships—and our view of God. We serve while silently suffering. We worship while deeply weary. We give endlessly while feeling disconnected.

But you are allowed to heal. You are allowed to grieve. You are allowed to *bring all of yourself* into the light of God's love.

Spiritual Care Practice: Grief Ritual – "I Release..."

Grief is not only for death. It's for the loss of innocence, safety, identity, belonging, and dreams. When we don't grieve, we carry those losses in silence—and that silence becomes misalignment.

Try This:

- Find a quiet place.

- On slips of paper, write the things you're ready to release.

    - *"I release the version of me who had to stay silent."*

    - *"I release the pressure to hold everyone together."*

    - *"I release the guilt I was never meant to carry."*

- Read them aloud. Burn, shred, or bury them in a symbolic act of release.

Let this become a sacred turning point, not a final one. Grief comes in waves—give yourself permission to feel it when it rises.

Practical Application: Compassion Over Correction

When your inner critic tries to shame you for still hurting or struggling, try this instead:

Compassion Exercise: Reparent Your Pain

Speak to yourself the way you would speak to a beloved child or friend.

- *"You're not wrong for feeling this way."*

- *"This pain makes sense."*

- *"You're doing the best you can."*

- *"God is not disappointed in you—He's present with you."*

This is how you begin to rewrite your inner narrative from shame to safety.

Mind-Body-Spirit Practice: Embodied Prayer – "God, Be With Me Here"

- Place one hand on your heart and one on your belly.
- Inhale deeply. Exhale slowly.
- Pray: *"God, be with me in my fear... in my grief... in my healing... in this moment."*

Repeat for 3–5 minutes. Let your body receive what your spirit already knows: you are held.

Emotional Resilience: You Don't Have to Be "Over It" to Be Healing

Healing is not linear. You don't graduate from grief. You don't "get over" trauma. You walk with it—honestly, gently, courageously.

You will have days where you feel whole and strong. And you'll have days where the ache returns. Neither one is a failure. Both are *part of your becoming*.

Malik's Grief Awakening

Malik had always been seen as a leader, a pillar in his family and community. But privately, he carried the weight of unresolved childhood trauma and the pain of losing his mother. When he finally gave himself permission to grieve—in silence, in tears, and in prayer—he felt peace for the first time in years. "I thought grief would break me," he said. "But it made me human again."

Sustainable Change: Tend What's Hidden—Slowly and Often

Make space for regular emotional and spiritual check-ins—not to perform healing, but to live from it.

Weekly Practice: Soul Tending Moment

- Set a 30-minute block. Light a candle.

- Ask:
    - *What needs my compassion this week?*
    - *What truth am I avoiding?*
    - *What memory or emotion needs acknowledgment, not analysis?*

Journal, pray, or simply sit with what rises. God will meet you there.

Community Engagement: #HealingWhatsHidden

This week, choose one practice—a grief ritual, breath prayer, or compassionate journal prompt—and share your experience with the hashtag **#HealingWhatsHidden**. Let others witness your courage and be encouraged by your honesty.

You don't have to keep carrying what you've never had space to name. You don't have to keep hiding the parts of you that still hurt. Your pain is not your identity. It's your invitation to return—to peace, to truth, to wholeness.

Healing isn't becoming someone new. It's returning to the parts of you that were always worthy of love.

Let's keep walking toward wholeness—one honest step at a time.

Reflection Questions

1. What pain or memory have you been avoiding or minimizing?
2. What emotions feel "unsafe" or too much for you to express?
3. How has your body been carrying the weight of your unspoken wounds?
4. What coping mechanisms have you used to manage pain instead of healing it?
5. What would it look like to offer compassion to the hurting parts of you?

You are not weak for feeling.
You are not broken for struggling.
You are not behind in your healing.

You are simply being invited to stop hiding—and start healing.

The God who created your soul is not waiting on your perfection.
He's waiting for your *permission*—to enter the places you've avoided, and to begin the slow, sacred work of making you whole.

A Prayer for Healing What's Hidden

God, there are places in me that I've been afraid to feel.
Wounds I've hidden beneath performance and pressure.
Emotions I've labeled "too much" or "too inconvenient."

But today, I choose honesty.
I choose to stop running.
I choose to feel, to name, to witness my pain.

I trust that You are not afraid of my broken places.
You're not in a hurry. You're not disappointed.

You are the Healer who enters the wound.
You are the Shepherd who sits with me in the valley.
You are the Truth that sets me free.

Help me heal—not by hiding, but by bringing it all into Your light.
Amen.

Chapter 6: Soul-Level Clarity in a World That Wants You Confused

"Noise is not neutral. It either draws you inward—or pulls you away from yourself."

We live in a world that profits off your confusion.

Let that sink in for a moment.

From the moment you wake up, you are pulled. Notifications light up your screen. Algorithms flood your feed. Opinions fill your ears. Expectations weigh on your shoulders. Everyone seems to have a message for you—telling you who you should be, what you should believe, how you should look, and what should matter most.

You don't even have to go looking for it.
It finds you.

And the result?
Many of us are spiritually *overstimulated*, emotionally *exhausted*, and mentally *disoriented*.

We're not short on information—we're drowning in it.
But what we're starving for is **clarity**.

Not the clarity that tells you how to master your morning routine or achieve your goals faster.

But the kind of soul-level clarity that grounds you in truth when everything around you feels chaotic.

The Battle for Your Attention

Your attention is sacred. It's one of the most powerful resources you have. And the world knows it.

Marketing agencies, social media platforms, news outlets, and even well-meaning influencers are all fighting for a piece of it. Their success often depends on your *distraction*, your *doubt*, and your *desire for more*.

Because when you're confused, you're more likely to consume.
When you're insecure, you're easier to influence.
When you're disoriented, you stop trusting your own voice.

It's not just noise—it's manipulation.
And it slowly pulls you away from the voice of God, from the truth of who you are, and from the stillness your soul desperately needs.

You're Not Lost—You're Just Distant from Yourself

So many people I counsel say things like:

- "I feel scattered all the time."

- "I can't tell if I'm hearing God or just overthinking."

- "I'm trying to stay grounded, but life feels like too much."

Here's what I want to tell you:

You're not broken—you're just out of sync.

The issue isn't your ability to hear from God or trust yourself. It's that the noise of life has gotten *louder* than the voice of truth.

And noise doesn't always look like chaos.
Sometimes it looks like:

- Constant productivity.

- Comparison masked as inspiration.

- Overcommitment dressed as obedience.

- Good advice that's not God's voice—for *you*.

The question isn't, "Am I listening?"
It's, "*What* am I listening to?"

What Soul Clarity Actually Is

Let's define what we're really talking about.

Soul clarity isn't about having every detail of your life mapped out.
It's not about knowing your five-year plan or crafting the perfect affirmation.

Soul clarity is about your mind, your will, and your emotions *knowing what's true*—about God, about yourself, and about what matters most.
It's the internal stillness that says:

- "This is who I am."

- "This is what I value."

- "This is the direction I'm being led."

- "This is what I need right now."

And it doesn't come through striving.
It comes through *stillness*, *discernment*, and *intentional presence*.

The Things That Distort Your Clarity

You can't protect what you don't recognize. So let's name the main forces that often distort soul clarity:

1. Chronic Comparison

We're inundated with images of other people's success, routines, aesthetics, and lives. Without realizing it, we start measuring our worth and decisions against someone else's curated version of life.

Clarity becomes clouded when you start asking, *"Am I doing enough?"* instead of *"Am I doing what aligns with my soul?"*

2. Overconsumption

When you're constantly taking in podcasts, videos, devotionals, sermons, and opinions, you don't leave space to actually *process* any of it.

Consumption without contemplation leads to confusion.

It's not about turning off truth—but about turning down the volume long enough to ask:
"What is God saying to me, specifically, in this season?"

3. Pleasing and Performing

Many of us have learned to base our direction on what others need or expect from us. We do what pleases people, earns applause, or checks the spiritual boxes—while quietly abandoning ourselves in the process.

But when you live by external affirmation, you will lose your internal clarity.

Creating Space for Clarity

The good news? You can reclaim your clarity. It hasn't been lost—it's just been buried.
Here are three ways to begin rebuilding a sacred rhythm that allows your soul to speak again.

---

1. Build Boundaries That Guard Your Attention

Boundaries are not barriers to connection—they are bridges to clarity.
You don't have to be available to everyone, all the time.
You don't have to consume everything that's "helpful."

Try this:

- **Digital boundaries**: Silence notifications during times of prayer, reflection, or rest.

- **Relational boundaries**: Create space from voices that consistently confuse or diminish your sense of identity.

- **Spiritual boundaries**: Choose depth over volume. Focus on one truth, one Scripture, or one reflection at a time.

Jesus often *withdrew to lonely places* to pray (Luke 5:16).
He didn't run on demand—He moved with discernment.

You're allowed to do the same.

---

2. Return to Rhythms of Stillness

Clarity doesn't scream—it whispers. And you can't hear a whisper in a noisy room.

You don't need a weekend retreat to find clarity. You need *moments* of intentional presence.

- Five minutes of silence in the morning before picking up your phone.

- Journaling a single question: "What am I feeling, and what do I need?"

- Taking a walk without music or input, just listening inward.

Stillness is not inactivity—it's *alignment*. It's the sacred practice of slowing down so you can tune in.

"Be still, and know that I am God."
(Psalm 46:10)

Stillness is where knowledge becomes *knowing*.
Where information becomes *intimacy*.

---

3. Cultivate Discernment Over Dependence

Many of us have been taught to trust spiritual leaders, programs, or content over our own discernment. While guidance is valuable, it should never replace your personal connection with God.

God speaks to *you*.
Your voice matters. Your discernment is developing. Your insight is valid.

You don't have to outsource your decisions. You don't have to second-guess every leading.

Start with this simple question:
"What aligns with the peace of God in me?"

Discernment grows with use. The more you pause, listen, and trust what you sense in God's presence, the clearer your inner compass becomes.

When Clarity Feels Far Away

There will be times when clarity feels distant—when your thoughts are cloudy, your emotions are heavy, and your direction feels murky.

In those moments, don't push harder.
Don't try to "figure it out" with your intellect alone.
Return to your center.

Remind yourself:

- *"I don't need all the answers to move forward."*

- *"God is not hiding from me."*

- *"Confusion is not my identity—clarity is my inheritance."*

Sometimes the clouds take time to clear. But the sun never left.
Your clarity will return—not through striving, but through *staying*.

You Deserve to Trust Yourself Again

If confusion has caused you to question your voice, your discernment, or your ability to hear from God, I want to remind you:

- You were made in God's image.

- You are filled with His Spirit.

- You have access to His wisdom.

You don't need to wait for external confirmation to validate your inner knowing.

Clarity comes when you begin to *believe* the truth that's already inside you.

How Culture, Capitalism, and Perfectionism Keep You Scattered

The world does not reward stillness. It rewards hustle. The systems many of us live and work within—capitalism, consumerism, perfectionism—thrive on your disconnection. When you don't know who you are or what you value, it's easier to sell you an identity, a product, or a performance.

Here's how these forces pull you out of alignment:

- **Culture** pressures you to keep up, look good, and stay relevant.
- **Capitalism** equates your worth with how much you produce.
- **Perfectionism** convinces you that love must be earned, not received.

These messages create chronic internal noise. But clarity doesn't come from doing more. It comes from *pausing long enough to listen within*.

Inner Exploration: Where Are You Scattered?

In a quiet moment, reflect:

- Where am I most easily pulled away from my peace?
- What messages have I internalized about success, worth, or value that don't align with my truth?
- Whose voice am I hearing most often—God's, mine, or someone else's?

Name what's noisy. Clarity often begins with subtraction.

Self-Assessment: Soul-Clarity Check-In

Rank the following from 1 (Strongly Disagree) to 5 (Strongly Agree):

1. I regularly create space to hear myself and God clearly.

2. I feel grounded in my values, even when life is busy.

3. I notice when I'm overconsuming noise or content.

4. I can say "no" without guilt when something doesn't align.

5. I know what matters most to me right now—and I live from it.

Interpretation:

- **5–10:** You're in a season of disconnection—begin to create intentional quiet space.

- **11–18:** You're aware of the noise, but need regular practices to return to your center.

- **19–25:** You're living with clarity—protect that alignment as life evolves.

Building Sacred Boundaries to Protect Your Focus

Boundaries are not about control—they're about clarity. They are how you protect your peace and preserve your ability to hear from God and yourself.

Start with these sacred boundaries:

- **Mental boundaries:** Limit how much information, advice, or media you consume.

- **Emotional boundaries:** Let go of the need to explain or defend your alignment to others.

- **Spiritual boundaries:** Guard your sacred space for prayer, rest, and stillness—without guilt.

You are allowed to protect your clarity. You are not being selfish. You're being *a good steward of your soul.*

Practical Application: The Sacred "No"

Every time you say yes to something that misaligns with your truth, you say no to your peace.

Try this practice:

1. Write down three "yeses" you've recently made that left you feeling drained or misaligned.

2. Ask:

    - Was I trying to be liked or avoid conflict?
    - Did I ignore what I knew was true?

3. Practice saying:

    - *"Thank you for thinking of me. I'm not available for that right now."*
    - *"That doesn't align with where I'm focusing this season."*

Say it out loud until it feels natural. Your boundaries are spiritual.

Spiritual Care Practice: Inner Listening – Hearing Yourself Again

Create a 10-minute sacred space this week to hear your own soul:

1. Sit in silence. No phone. No music.
2. Breathe deeply. Place your hand on your heart.
3. Ask: *What do I need right now? What's trying to speak through the silence?*
4. Write down what rises—without editing or spiritualizing it.

You are not looking for answers. You're looking for presence.

Mind-Body-Spirit Practice: Somatic Grounding for Clarity

Try this simple grounding practice when you feel overwhelmed or unclear:

- Place your feet flat on the ground.

- Name 5 things you see, 4 things you feel, 3 things you hear, 2 things you smell, 1 truth you know.

- End with: *"God is here. I am here. I am listening."*

This anchors your body in the present and creates space for soul-level clarity to emerge.

Emotional Resilience: When Others Don't Understand Your Alignment

As you begin to live with more clarity and intention, some people may not understand your new boundaries, slower pace, or deeper "no." That's okay.

Clarity often requires *courage*—the courage to disappoint others in order to remain faithful to yourself and to God.

Here's what I want you to remember:

- You are not responsible for managing other people's discomfort with your growth.

- You are not abandoning others by choosing to live from your truth.

- Clarity is a gift to you *and* to the people you're called to serve.

Janelle's Sacred "Yes"

Janelle, an entrepreneur and a community leader, was constantly exhausted. "I didn't realize how much I was saying 'yes' to things that weren't mine to carry," she told me. Through inner listening and value work, she identified her deepest priority—*peace*. She began scheduling silence into her mornings and saying no to non-essential meetings. "The clarity didn't come from a course," she said. "It came from getting quiet. From returning to myself."

Sustainable Change: Daily and Seasonal Clarity Practices

Daily: Ask yourself each morning,

- *What matters most to me today?*

- *What noise do I need to turn down?*

Monthly: Set aside 30–60 minutes to reflect, realign, and reset.

- What's been scattering my energy?

- What's emerging that I need to prioritize?

- What do I need more—or less—of?

Let these rhythms become a spiritual maintenance plan for your soul.

Community Engagement: #SoulClarityChallenge

For the next 7 days, spend 10 minutes each morning in silence before consuming any content. Listen inward. Journal one word, phrase, or insight.

Share using the hashtag **#SoulClarityChallenge** to encourage others who are tuning back into their own inner voice.

You were never meant to live in confusion. You were made to live with clarity—gentle, grounded, soul-level clarity that flows from the Spirit of God within you. You don't need to chase it. You only need to make space for it.

You are allowed to live a quiet, aligned life—even when the world wants you loud and busy.

You're hearing yourself again. And that's where healing begins.

A Prayer for Clarity

> God, I've been pulled in so many directions.
> The noise of life has crowded out Your whisper.
> I've looked to everyone else for answers—
> and neglected the voice You placed within me.
>
> Today, I choose stillness.
> I choose to unplug from noise and return to Presence.

Remind me that I don't need to strive for clarity—
I simply need to create space for it.

Help me hear again.
Not the loudest voice, but the truest one.
Not the world's direction, but Yours.
I trust that Your wisdom is already at work in me.
Amen.

Part 3: Becoming Whole – Alignment in Daily Life

Chapter 7: From Knowing to Becoming – Embodying the True Self

"You don't need more insight. You need embodiment. You need to become what you already believe."

By now, you likely know more about yourself than you did when you started this journey.

You've named your hidden pain.
You've learned to listen to your soul.
You've reconnected to your values, your voice, your vision.
You've begun to shed the false self, question the noise, and pursue alignment.

That is sacred work. It is holy ground. And if no one has told you—*I'm proud of you.*

But there's a place in the healing journey where many people stop.
It's not because they're weak. It's not because they've failed.
It's because this next step requires more than reflection—it requires *transformation*.

It's the step from *knowing* to *becoming*.

Why Insight Isn't Enough

Insight is powerful.
It helps us see clearly.
It awakens compassion.
It gives language to what once felt confusing.

But insight without embodiment leads to frustration.

- You can know you need rest—and still never take it.

- You can know you're worthy—and still sabotage your success.

- You can know your boundaries matter—and still let them collapse at the first pushback.

Knowing is necessary.
But it's *not the destination*.
The goal isn't just to have new thoughts—it's to live a new life.

> "Do not merely listen to the word, and so deceive yourselves. Do what it says."
> (James 1:22)

Becoming is where wholeness becomes visible. It's where your internal healing starts to shape your external reality. Not just in what you say, but in how you *show up*.

The Gap Between Awareness and Action

In spiritual care, I often see people hit what I call the "integration gap." It's that space between:

- *I know what I need...*

- ...and *I'm actually living like it.*

It's one thing to understand your story. It's another thing to *walk in freedom from it.*
It's one thing to write a new affirmation. It's another thing to *believe it at the cellular level.*

Why is this gap so hard to cross?

Because embodiment feels *vulnerable*. It makes the healing real.
It moves you from safe contemplation into messy, courageous practice.

And practice—real, lived practice—will expose every part of you still learning to believe what you now *know.*

Becoming Is Not Performance

Let me be clear: becoming your true self is not about perfection or performance.
It's not about looking more spiritual, or pretending your growth is linear.
It's not about proving your healing.

Becoming is about *alignment*—bringing your daily actions, habits, and relationships into harmony with the truth God has revealed to you.

It looks like:

- Saying "no" when you used to people-please.

- Resting on purpose, even when guilt knocks at your door.

- Showing up honestly in spaces where you once hid behind a mask.

- Letting your voice be heard, even when your hands are shaking.

You don't need a perfect plan. You need *permission* to practice being *you*.

From Belief to Behavior

Let's break it down even more.

There is a clear progression in healing:

1. **Revelation** – You realize what's misaligned.

2. **Reflection** – You explore why it happened and what it's cost you.

3. **Realignment** – You choose what needs to shift.

4. **Rhythm** – You begin embodying those shifts in your daily life.

That last one is the key.
Because transformation doesn't stick through occasional epiphanies.
It sticks through *consistent embodiment*.

It shows up in your:

- Morning routine
- Conversations
- Calendar

- Boundaries
- Budget
- Relationships
- Spiritual practices

Every part of your life becomes an expression of your healing—or your disconnection.
The more aligned you are internally, the more integrity you live with externally.

Embodiment Is a Form of Worship

Living your truth isn't just self-care. It's *spiritual obedience*.

> *"Therefore, I urge you... to offer your bodies as a living sacrifice, holy and pleasing to God—this is your true and proper worship." (Romans 12:1)*

Notice the language—**your body**.
Not just your spirit. Not just your beliefs.
Your whole being.

When you embody peace instead of panic,
When you walk in truth instead of pretending,
When you speak from wholeness instead of hiding—
You are worshiping God with your *life*.

Becoming is not about becoming someone *new*—
It's about returning to who you were always meant to be.

It Will Feel Uncomfortable—And That's Okay

Embodiment feels risky at first.

- The first time you rest when you're used to overworking.
- The first time you tell the truth instead of what's expected.
- The first time you let yourself be seen in your softness, not just your strength.

You'll feel resistance. That's normal.
Your nervous system is adjusting.
Your habits are recalibrating.
Your inner critic may scream, "Who do you think you are?"

But the discomfort of becoming is temporary.
The peace it unlocks is *permanent*.

Creating Embodied Rhythms

So what does this look like in practical terms?

Let's explore three areas of life where you can begin embodying your true self today:

1. Time: How You Spend Your Day

How you structure your time reveals what you value—whether consciously or not.

Start small:

- Schedule space for stillness—not just when you crash, but on purpose.

- Block time for creative work that aligns with your purpose.

- Let your calendar reflect your healing—not just your hustle.

---

2. Relationships: How You Show Up With Others

Do your relationships allow you to be your true self? Do you still feel the need to perform?

Embodying your truth may mean:

- Having honest conversations you've been avoiding.

- Saying "I'm not okay" instead of pretending.

- Allowing people to love the *real* you—not just the version you've curated.

---

3. Body: How You Treat and Trust It

Your body carries your story.
It also becomes the place where healing can finally land.

Practice embodiment through:

- Breathwork or movement that brings you back to yourself.
- Eating in ways that nourish—not punish—your body.
- Resting *before* you hit burnout.

The body is not the enemy of your healing—it's the *partner* in your transformation.

Becoming the Type of Person Who...

When people feel stuck, I often offer this gentle prompt:

> "What would it look like to become the type of person who lives aligned?"

Not *perfectly*, but *authentically*.

- The type of person who speaks up when something feels wrong.
- The type of person who no longer over-functions in relationships.
- The type of person who moves through the world with peace, not pressure.
- The type of person who receives love without needing to earn it.

This is where embodiment begins—not with a perfect life, but with a *real one*.

Grace for the Becoming

Please don't rush this process.

You are not behind because you're still learning.
You're not failing because you still fall back into old habits.
Becoming is not linear—it's layered.

Some days you will live aligned.
Other days you will feel like you've forgotten everything you've learned.

But grace walks with you.
Every step. Every stumble. Every stretch.

The Power of Repetition

Embodiment happens not in *what you try once*, but in *what you return to daily*.

You don't become free by thinking about freedom.
You become free by *practicing* freedom.

You don't become peaceful by reading about peace.
You become peaceful by *choosing* it—over and over again.

Repetition is not failure—it's *formation*.

Becoming Is Contagious

Here's what I've seen over and over again:
When you embody your healing, other people feel it.

Your presence becomes safe.
Your peace becomes contagious.
Your authenticity becomes an invitation for others to do the same.

You don't have to preach your transformation.
You *are* the message.

And that message is this:
It's safe to be who God created you to be.

The Difference Between Awareness and Embodiment

Let's get clear:

- **Awareness** says, "I know what I need."

- **Embodiment** says, "I'm living like I believe I deserve it."

- **Awareness** observes the wound.

- **Embodiment** learns to walk differently because of the healing.

Knowing is where you start. Embodying is where you shift.

This is where we move from theory to transformation.

Inner Exploration: What Truth Am I Not Yet Living?

Take a breath. Grab your journal and reflect:

- What is something I *know* about myself, my values, or my calling—but haven't made space to *live*?

- What keeps me stuck in planning or talking instead of doing?

- What would shift in my life if I embodied that truth daily?

Be honest. You're not being judged. You're being invited.

Self-Assessment: Embodiment Inventory

Rate each of the following from 1 (Never) to 5 (Always):

1. My daily habits reflect what I say I value.

2. I take time to reconnect with myself, not just perform for others.

3. I follow through on what I say I want for my life.

4. I don't just process emotions—I allow them to move through me.

5. I live with a rhythm that supports my mental, emotional, and spiritual well-being.

Scoring:

- **5–10:** You're collecting knowledge—now it's time to translate that into aligned action.

- **11–18:** You're practicing embodiment—keep nurturing the shifts.

- **19–25:** You're walking your truth—protect this space and remain rooted.

Creating Rhythms of Alignment: Spiritual Disciplines for Real Life

You don't need a monastery or a sabbatical to live aligned. You need rhythm. And you need to believe that small, consistent practices are more powerful than occasional spiritual highs.

Here are simple, sustainable rhythms of embodiment:

- **Morning Centering:** Breath prayer. Scripture meditation. Silence before screens.

- **Midday Check-In:** One deep breath. One honest question: *"What do I need right now?"*

- **Evening Reset:** Journal a moment of alignment and a moment of misalignment. Offer it all back to God.

These aren't rules. They're rituals that help you return to yourself.

Practical Application: Micro-Alignments for Busy Days

Let's be real—life is full. But you don't need hours of margin to live aligned. You just need intentional *moments*.

Try these micro-alignments:

- **5-second prayer:** *"God, center me in truth."*

- **2-minute journaling prompt:** *"What feels like peace today?"*

- **Intentional breath:** Inhale *"I am safe,"* exhale *"I am present."*

- **Daily question:** *"Does this choice reflect the life I say I want?"*

Over time, these small practices rewire how you *live*, not just how you *think*.

Spiritual Care Practice: Rhythm Mapping

Take a piece of paper. Divide it into four sections:

- Morning
- Midday
- Evening
- Night

Under each, write one small practice you could use to support alignment in that window of your day.

Example:

- **Morning:** Read one verse + silent prayer
- **Midday:** 10-minute walk without phone
- **Evening:** Honest journaling
- **Night:** Stretch and breath prayer before bed

Start simple. Make it yours.

Mind-Body-Spirit Practice: Embodied Prayer Ritual

Use this when you feel disconnected or disoriented.

1. Stand or sit in a quiet space.
2. Raise your arms as you inhale: *"God, I receive Your peace."*
3. Cross your arms over your chest: *"I return to myself."*
4. Bow your head: *"I walk aligned today."*

Let your *body* pray what your words may not yet know how to say.

Emotional Resilience: Becoming Without Burning Out

Embodiment is not about perfection. It's about presence. You will have days when you fall out of rhythm. Don't shame yourself. Realignment is always one breath, one prayer, one decision away.

When self-doubt creeps in, remember:

- It's not too late to become who you truly are.

- You don't have to do it all today.

- You are already worthy of a life that feels like peace.

Malik's Shift from Awareness to Action

Malik had done the soul work—journaling, therapy, reading. But he still felt off. "I *knew* what needed to change," he told me. "But I kept putting it off because I didn't know where to start."

He began with one new rhythm: 20 minutes of solitude each morning. That small act led to clearer boundaries, more meaningful prayer, and deeper presence with his family. "The clarity didn't come from more doing," he said. "It came from finally living what I already knew."

Sustainable Change: Building Your Embodiment Plan

Your alignment needs structure. Not rigidity—*support.*

Choose Your Daily Anchors:

- **Anchor 1: Morning Presence**
  (Ex: Breath prayer + Scripture)

- **Anchor 2: Midday Reset**
  (Ex: Silence + values check-in)

- **Anchor 3: Evening Reflection**
  (Ex: Gratitude + alignment review)

Monthly Check-In:

- What rhythms are supporting my alignment?

- What needs to be adjusted?

- Am I *living* what I say I believe?

Community Engagement: #EmbodyMyTruth

Choose one embodied practice and commit to it for 7 days. Share your experience using the hashtag **#EmbodyMyTruth**. Your becoming will inspire others to return to themselves, too.

You don't need to earn the right to live aligned. You're allowed to begin now. Not when life slows down. Not when it's perfect. But today.

You don't need to perform your transformation.
You just need to live from it.
With presence.
With grace.
With peace.

Let's keep becoming. From the inside out.

Reflection Questions

1. Where in your life do you feel a gap between what you know and how you live?

2. What does your current schedule, routine, or rhythm say about what you believe?

3. What's one small habit you could shift this week to reflect your values more fully?

4. What makes embodiment feel scary or unfamiliar for you?

5. Who in your life supports and celebrates the version of you that's becoming more whole?

Knowing is the first step. Becoming is the journey.

You are not here to just *understand* alignment.
You're here to *embody* it.

And with every step you take—however small—you are walking in truth, walking in freedom, and walking in the fullness of who you were created to be.

A Prayer for Becoming

> God, I've spent so long learning, reading, processing...
> And now You're inviting me to *live* what I've learned.
>
> I don't want to stop at insight. I want embodiment.
> I want to walk like someone who is whole.
> I want to move like someone who is loved.
> I want to rest like someone who is free.
>
> Help me show up in truth—even when it's hard.
> Help me live aligned—even when it's unfamiliar.
> Let my habits reflect my healing.
> Let my rhythms reflect Your grace.
>
> I am becoming—and You are with me every step.
> Amen.

Chapter 8: Inner Peace as a Practice, Not a Place

"Peace I leave with you; my peace I give you. I do not give to you as the world gives." – John 14:27

We talk about peace like it's a destination.
Something we'll arrive at *when life finally calms down*.
When our inbox is empty.
When our children are behaving.
When our body feels better.
When the to-do list is finally done.
When everyone else is happy and we've somehow managed to fix the world around us.

But here's the truth: **that kind of peace is an illusion.**
It's fragile. Fleeting.
And it places your well-being in the hands of everything you cannot control.

The peace your soul was made for is different.
It's not circumstantial—it's **spiritual**.
It's not passive—it's **a practice**.
It doesn't depend on what's happening around you.
It flows from what's happening *within you*.

> "Peace I leave with you; my peace I give you."
> (John 14:27)

Jesus didn't promise a peaceful world. He promised *His* peace.
And that peace is not a place you visit—it's a **presence** you carry.

We've Been Taught to Chase Peace

From an early age, we're conditioned to believe that peace is something we earn.

- If you work hard enough, you'll find rest.
- If you fix all the problems, you'll feel better.
- If you finally get control, you'll feel calm.

So we chase it:

- Through performance.
- Through productivity.
- Through perfectionism.
- Through people-pleasing.

But the more we chase, the more elusive peace becomes. Because peace was never meant to be pursued from the *outside in*.
It was always meant to be cultivated from the *inside out*.

Peace Is Not the Absence of Chaos

One of the greatest lies we've believed is that peace equals stillness in our circumstances.
That when things are "normal" or "quiet," then we'll feel peace.

But real peace isn't the absence of noise, conflict, or pressure.
It's the presence of *God* in the middle of it.

Peace says:

- "Even here, I'm anchored."

- "Even now, I'm okay."

- "Even in this, I trust."

You won't always be able to silence the world around you.
But you can cultivate a stillness within you that remains unshaken by what's outside.

What Robs Us of Peace?

Peace doesn't disappear randomly. It gets slowly *eroded*.
Often, not by catastrophe—but by a thousand little compromises.

Here are just a few of the peace-robbers we often overlook:

1. Mental Clutter

Endless thoughts, what-ifs, worst-case scenarios, self-criticism, and overanalysis.

Your mind becomes so loud that your spirit has no space to speak.

2. Unrealistic Expectations

The belief that you must be everything to everyone. That rest is earned. That slowing down is laziness.

3. Overconsumption

Too much news. Too much scrolling. Too much advice. Even too much spiritual input—if it replaces stillness with stimulation.

4. Unprocessed Emotions

Avoided grief, denied anger, buried anxiety. Emotions don't vanish—they wait.

5. Disconnection from God

When time with God becomes a task rather than a relationship, we lose our source of peace.

Peace Is a Spiritual Rhythm

Instead of treating peace like a reward for "getting it all right," what if you treated it like a **rhythm**? A sacred rhythm you return to, again and again, as part of your daily life.

Peace is not a feeling you wait for—it's a **muscle** you build.

You build it by returning to stillness.
You build it by listening inward.
You build it by recognizing what's robbing you—and gently releasing it.

Let's explore how.

---

1. Anchor Your Day in Stillness

You don't need an hour-long morning routine to experience peace.
You just need *intentional stillness*.

- A few minutes of quiet before your day begins.

- A breath prayer before answering emails.

- Sitting with your coffee in silence—not multitasking, just *being*.

Stillness isn't a luxury. It's a lifeline.
It's where you center your soul before the world tries to scatter you.

> "Be still, and know that I am God."
> *(Psalm 46:10)*

Stillness reminds you: you are not what you do.
You are not what you produce.
You are held. You are safe. You are anchored.

---

2. Practice Gentle Re-centering

Peace doesn't mean you never get off track. It means you *notice* when you do—and gently return.

Throughout your day, ask:

- *What's pulling me out of peace?*
- *What do I need to release?*
- *Where is God in this moment?*

Sometimes the answer is to take a break.
Sometimes it's to speak up.
Sometimes it's to let something go that was never yours to carry.

This is the work of practicing peace—not perfectly, but consistently.

---

3. Listen to Your Body's Signals

Your body often knows you're not at peace before your mind does.

- Tension in your jaw or shoulders.
- A racing heart.
- Shallow breathing.
- Chronic fatigue.

These aren't signs of failure. They're invitations to *pause*.
Your body is asking you to return—to breath, to rest, to Presence.

Peace is not just a spiritual concept.
It's a *physiological experience.*
When you embody peace, your body begins to trust that it's safe.

---

4. Silence the Inner Noise

Some of the loudest noise isn't from the outside—it's from within.

- The voice that says you're not doing enough.
- The fear that you'll be forgotten if you slow down.
- The anxiety that tells you something must be wrong if you're not rushing.

These voices are often rooted in old stories, trauma, or fear.
But they are not the voice of God.

> "The Lord will fight for you; you need only to be still."
> *(Exodus 14:14)*

God's voice brings peace—even when it convicts.
It does not agitate. It does not shame.
You can trust the voice that speaks in *stillness and love.*

---

5. Protect Your Peace Like It's Sacred—Because It Is

You have a right to protect your peace.
You don't have to explain your boundaries.
You don't have to apologize for taking time to rest, reset, or say no.

Peace is not selfish—it's spiritual stewardship.
When you protect your peace, you protect your ability to love well, serve well, and live well.

Ask yourself:

- What conversations, environments, or habits regularly rob me of peace?
- What would it look like to give myself permission to choose peace over performance?

Sometimes the most courageous thing you can do is protect your *quiet* in a world that demands your noise.

Peace Doesn't Mean Everything's Perfect

One of the lies we believe is that "when I have peace, nothing will bother me."

No. You're still human.

Peace doesn't mean you never get upset, overwhelmed, or anxious.
It means you *notice* sooner.
It means you *recover* faster.
It means you're no longer swept away by every emotional storm.

Peace gives you the inner capacity to hold your ground, even when life tries to shake it.

Returning to the Peace Already Within You

Here's the most beautiful part:
You don't have to go find peace.
Peace is *already in you.*

Jesus said, *"My peace I give you."*

It's a gift. A presence. A well within your soul.
You just have to return to it.

- When life gets loud—return.

- When your thoughts spiral—return.

- When anxiety creeps in—return.

- When everything feels too heavy—return.

Return to breath.
Return to Presence.
Return to the truth that peace is not a destination.
It is your *birthright as a child of God.*

Why Peace Isn't Passive—It's Courageous

In a culture that glorifies hustle, performance, and perfection, choosing peace is an act of holy rebellion. It takes *courage* to pause when everyone else is running. It takes *strength* to release control when your anxiety says you can't. And it takes *faith* to trust that God's presence is enough—even when nothing around you changes.

Peace doesn't mean life is easy. It means you're *anchored* in the storm, not ruled by it.

Inner Exploration: What Is Stealing Your Peace?

Grab your journal or sit in stillness with God. Ask:

- Where am I most unsettled right now?

- What pressure am I carrying that isn't mine to hold?

- Whose voice am I hearing louder than God's?

- What would choosing peace look like in my current season?

Let honesty lead. Peace is found in truth, not performance.

Self-Assessment: Inner Peace Inventory

Rate from 1 (Strongly Disagree) to 5 (Strongly Agree):

1. I regularly experience a sense of internal calm or stillness.

2. I take time to rest and recharge without guilt.

3. I can notice anxious thoughts without being controlled by them.

4. I have practices that help me return to peace when I feel overwhelmed.

5. I give myself grace instead of judgment when I fall short.

Scoring:

- **5–10:** You're longing for peace—start with gentle stillness and compassionate rhythms.

- **11–18:** You're building peace—nurture consistency and space.

- **19–25:** You are living anchored—keep protecting this peace.

Releasing the Inner Critic and Perfectionism

One of the greatest enemies of peace isn't chaos—it's your inner critic. That voice that says:

- "You should be further along."

- "You didn't do enough today."

- "You can't rest until everything's done."

Perfectionism robs you of rest and convinces you that peace must be earned. But the gospel says otherwise.

You don't have to hustle to be holy.
You don't have to be perfect to be whole.

Peace isn't proof that you have everything together. It's the fruit of living *connected*—to God, to yourself, and to what matters most.

Practical Application: Cultivating Peace on Purpose

These practices aren't magic. They're muscles—built through repetition, grace, and presence.

1. Breath Prayers

Use your breath to ground yourself in God's nearness.

- Inhale: *"You are with me..."*

- Exhale: *"...and I am safe."*

Repeat slowly for 2–5 minutes.

2. Stillness Moments

Create quiet micro-pauses in your day. No phone. No input. Just presence.

- 3 minutes.

- Sit or lie down.

- Say: *"This moment is enough. I am enough."*

Let yourself just *be*—without needing to produce, fix, or plan.

3. Somatic Settling

Peace isn't just a mindset—it's a body state.

Try This Grounding Practice:

- Place both feet flat on the ground.

- Press fingertips together gently.

- Name: 5 things you see, 4 things you feel, 3 things you hear, 2 things you smell, 1 truth you know.

- Breathe deeply and repeat: *"I am here. God is here."*

Mind-Body-Spirit Practice: "The Peace Chair"

Choose a physical space—a chair, corner, or cushion—that becomes your sacred peace space. Let it symbolize your commitment to stillness, presence, and internal safety.

Each time you sit there:

- Leave your to-do list at the door.

- Speak kindly to yourself.

- Invite God into your breath, body, and being.

Let your nervous system learn: *peace is safe. Peace is allowed.*

Emotional Resilience: When Peace Feels Out of Reach

You won't always feel peaceful. You'll have anxious thoughts. Sleepless nights. Situations that shake you.

That doesn't mean peace is gone. It means peace needs to be *practiced*.

When your body is tense and your mind is racing:

- Pause.

- Breathe.

- Whisper: *"Peace is possible, even here."*

Return again and again. Not because you failed—but because you're human.

Brianna's Return to Peace

Brianna, a single mom of three, came to one of my spiritual care groups overwhelmed and worn down. "I can't remember the last time I felt peace," she admitted. We didn't start with theology or tools—we started with one stillness moment a day.

Five minutes. Just her breath, her body, and a single prayer: *"Be with me here, God."*

Two weeks later, she said, "My life hasn't changed. But something inside me has. I finally feel like I can breathe."

That's peace.

Sustainable Change: Designing Your Peace Practice

Step 1: Choose a Daily Anchor

- Breath prayer, silent sit, gentle walk, or body scan

- 5–10 minutes. Protect it like your peace depends on it—because it does.

Step 2: Name Your Triggers

- Where does anxiety spike?

- What people, spaces, or tasks pull you from center?

- Create a response plan: a breath, a prayer, a pause.

Step 3: Return Often

- When you fall out of rhythm, don't start over.

- Just return. One breath, one prayer, one moment at a time.

Community Engagement: #PracticePeace Challenge

Commit to one peace practice every day for 7 days. Share what helped you reconnect, slow down, or breathe again using the hashtag **#PracticePeace**. Let peace become something we build together.

You are allowed to feel safe in your body.
You are allowed to rest without guilt.
You are allowed to stop performing and start *receiving*.

Peace is not something you wait for.
It's something you *practice*—on purpose, with grace.

And every time you choose peace, you return to yourself—and to God.

Reflection Questions

1. How have you been taught to think about peace? Is it something you chase or something you cultivate?

2. What are the internal or external sources of noise that consistently pull you away from peace?

3. What signals does your body give you when you're not at peace?

4. What small practice—breathing, silence, prayer, journaling—helps you reconnect with peace?

5. What would it look like to treat peace as a spiritual rhythm instead of a finish line?

You don't have to wait for life to calm down to feel peace.
You don't have to fix everything to breathe deeply.
You don't have to be perfect to feel grounded.

You can choose peace right here, right now—because the Prince of Peace lives in you.

It won't always feel natural at first.
But over time, as you return again and again to stillness, peace will stop feeling like a place you visit...
And start becoming the *home* you carry wherever you go.

A Prayer for Peace

> God, I've been chasing peace like it's a place—
> Something I'll reach when everything is finally okay.
>
> But today, I hear Your voice saying:
> *Peace is already within you.*
>
> Help me stop running and start *returning*.
>
> Quiet the noise—outside and within.
> Show me what's pulling me away.
> Remind me that peace isn't the absence of problems—
> It's the presence of You.
>
> Let me breathe in Your stillness.
> Let me move from Your center.
> Let peace become my practice, not just my prayer.
> Amen.

Chapter 9: Building a Life That Feels Like You

"You weren't created to perform life. You were created to live it—on purpose, from the inside out."

Misalignment doesn't always show up in chaos.
Sometimes, it shows up in a beautiful home you no longer feel at home in.
In a full calendar that leaves no space for your soul.
In accolades that don't match your inner sense of peace.
In a life that looks "successful" on the outside—but feels hollow inside.

You're doing all the "right" things—serving, leading, showing up.
You're present—but disconnected.
You're producing—but not fulfilled.
You're accomplishing—but you don't feel *alive*.

That's when the whisper begins:
There has to be more than this.

And there is.
But not "more" as in *more to do*.
"More" as in *more aligned. More whole. More you.*

The Wake-Up Call of Misalignment

There comes a moment for all of us when we realize we've been building a life around the wrong blueprint.

Maybe you inherited expectations.
Maybe you built your life around survival.
Maybe you've been reacting to fear or pain rather than responding to vision.

Whatever the case, something inside you knows: *this isn't sustainable*. And more than that, *this isn't who I truly am*.

This chapter is an invitation to pause long enough to ask:

- *What kind of life am I really building?*

- *And does it reflect who I truly am—or just who I've been expected to be?*

A Life That *Feels* Like You

Let's be clear: this isn't about perfection.
This isn't about building a picture-perfect life, complete with the ideal schedule, curated aesthetic, and flawless routines.

This is about **integrity**—not moral perfection, but *wholeness*.
It's about your life feeling like a reflection of your spirit.
It's about living in a way that allows you to exhale instead of constantly performing.

A life that feels like you is:

- Rooted in your values.

- Informed by your vision.

- Guided by your voice.

- Aligned with God's presence.

This is not a fantasy. It's possible. But it requires intention.

You don't drift into a meaningful life. You **design** it—on purpose, from the inside out.

Letting Go of the Life You "Should" Have

Before you can build a life that feels like you, you may need to grieve the one that doesn't.

That might mean letting go of:

- Roles that no longer reflect your season.

- Expectations that were never yours to carry.

- Dreams that belonged to a version of you that's no longer here.

- Structures that kept you performing but not thriving.

This kind of release isn't failure—it's *faithfulness* to your soul.

Just because something once worked for you doesn't mean it still serves you. And just because something served a purpose in one season doesn't mean it belongs in the next.

Reclaiming Your Blueprint

You were created with a divine design. Not a formula. Not a prescription. A **blueprint** that reflects the heart of God and the truth of who you are.

That blueprint is not external. It's internal.

- Your **values** are the foundation.
- Your **voice** is the guide.
- Your **vision** is the architecture.
- Your **habits** are the bricks.
- And God is the builder, co-laboring with you every step of the way.

> *"Unless the Lord builds the house, the builders labor in vain."*
> *(Psalm 127:1)*

This is the sacred shift: moving from performing life to *living* it—intentionally, authentically, and aligned with who God created you to be.

Step One: Recenter on Your Values

Values are the truths you want your life to embody—*not just believe, but live.*

They're the compass that guides your decisions, your energy, your boundaries. Without clear values, you will default to the loudest voices around you—culture, fear, guilt, or obligation.

Take a moment to ask:

- What matters most to me in this season?

- When do I feel most aligned, most alive?

- What have I been saying "yes" to that violates what I truly value?

Maybe your value is **authentic connection**, but your life is dominated by shallow relationships.
Maybe your value is **rest**, but you've been glorifying hustle.
Maybe your value is **God's presence**, but your schedule leaves no time to be still.

Clarity here is the foundation for everything else.

Step Two: Rebuild Your Rhythms

Once you're clear on your values, it's time to **build rhythms that reflect them.**

This is where your life begins to *feel* different—not because everything changes overnight, but because you begin to move with **integrity**.

Start simple.

If you value **peace**, create quiet space each morning.
If you value **family**, block out undistracted time.
If you value **growth**, protect time for reading, learning, or reflecting.

Don't let your calendar contradict your soul.

Your time is a mirror of what you truly believe is important.
When you align your rhythms with your values, your life starts to feel like a home—not a stage.

Step Three: Reclaim Your Voice in Every Room

Building a life that feels like you requires your **voice**.

Not the voice that keeps others comfortable.
Not the voice shaped by performance.
But the voice that tells the truth—your truth.

Your voice matters in:

- Your relationships: Are you showing up honestly?

- Your career or calling: Are you aligned with your purpose?

- Your community: Are you hiding parts of yourself to belong?

Living a life that feels like you means showing up as *you*.
And that's not always easy—but it is freeing.

God doesn't bless the version of you you're pretending to be.
He blesses the one He *created*.

Step Four: Align Your Vision With God's Heart

Sometimes, we confuse "big vision" with "big performance." But vision doesn't have to be flashy to be faithful.

Maybe your vision is a peaceful home, not a platform.
Maybe it's nurturing a community, not leading a movement.
Maybe it's living simply, loving deeply, and walking humbly with God.

Big or small, *vision matters*.
And it should come from God's heart, not cultural pressure.

Ask Him:

- What kind of life do You want to build in and through me?

- What does wholeness look like in *my* season?

- What kind of legacy do You want me to leave?

When you align your life with *God's* vision for *you*, everything changes—not because it gets easier, but because it finally makes sense.

Step Five: Let It Be Unapologetically Yours

A life that feels like you will not always be understood.
It may not be impressive to others.
It may be quieter, slower, or simpler than what people expect.

But if it's aligned? If it reflects your values, voice, and vision?
It's *holy*.

You're not here to live a life that looks good on Instagram.
You're here to live a life that feels good in your soul.

That means:

- Choosing alignment over approval.
- Choosing peace over performance.
- Choosing purpose over pressure.

What If You're Not There Yet?

You may be thinking: *I don't even know what a life that feels like me looks like anymore.*

That's okay.

This is not a race. It's a return.

- Return to your center.
- Return to Presence.
- Return to what you know is true—even if you can't live it fully yet.

God isn't asking you to have it all figured out.
He's inviting you to rebuild—brick by brick, moment by moment.

You don't need perfection. You need permission.
To pause.
To pivot.
To begin again.

A Life That Feels Like You—Because It's Rooted in Him

Ultimately, a life that feels like you is one that's rooted in **Christ in you**.

Not the culture's version of success.
Not even your own best plans.
But the Spirit of God, alive in your everyday life.

> *"In Him we live and move and have our being."*
> *(Acts 17:28)*

That's the key.
Not just a life that reflects *you*—but one that reflects the *you* God created.

When your soul is aligned with His Spirit, your life doesn't just feel "successful."
It feels *sacred*.

Redesigning from the Inside Out

Many of us inherited lives without realizing it—patterns, roles, habits, and responsibilities that were passed down, assumed, or accumulated out of survival. But what got you here isn't always what will sustain you in your next season.

You were never meant to build a life by default. You were meant to *design* one by discernment.

To build a life that feels like you, you must start from the inside out:

- **Who are you becoming?**

- **What do you value most?**

- **What kind of pace, presence, and peace do you want to carry?**

When your life reflects your truth, you don't have to fight for peace. You *live* in it.

Inner Exploration: Is My Life Reflecting My Truth?

In stillness or through journaling, reflect on:

- Which parts of my life feel most misaligned with who I am?

- Where have I said yes out of guilt instead of alignment?

- If I could start fresh, what would I choose to carry—and what would I release?

This is not about shame. It's about clarity. And clarity leads to freedom.

Self-Assessment: Life Alignment Snapshot

Evaluate each area on a scale of 1 (Completely Misaligned) to 5 (Deeply Aligned):

1. My daily schedule reflects my core values.

2. My work or service aligns with my purpose.

3. My relationships are mutual, nourishing, and life-giving.

4. I have space for rest, creativity, and joy.

5. I feel a sense of peace and congruence in my life.

Interpretation:

- **5–10:** Misalignment is draining your energy—small shifts will make a big difference.

- **11–18:** You're on the path—time to refine and realign with more intention.

- **19–25:** You're living your truth—protect that space with sacred boundaries.

Life Integration Map: The Four Cs

Use this framework to explore the four key domains that shape a whole life:

1. Career/Purpose

- Am I using my gifts in meaningful ways?
- Do I feel purposeful in how I show up daily?

2. Creativity

- Where do I express myself freely, without productivity pressure?
- What used to bring me joy that I've stopped doing?

3. Community

- Who truly sees and supports me?
- Where am I staying connected out of obligation?

4. Care (for Self & Spirit)

- Do I feel nourished—physically, emotionally, spiritually?
- What replenishes me? What drains me?

Map your answers in a journal or visual chart. This becomes your *life design blueprint.*

What Aligned Decision-Making Actually Looks Like

Living aligned doesn't mean you never struggle—it means you make decisions from your center, not your fear.

The Aligned Decision Model

Pause.
Don't rush. Create sacred space before reacting.

Pray.
Ask God: *"Does this decision reflect who You created me to be?"*

Process.
Ask yourself:

- Is this rooted in love or fear?
- Does it support my peace, or sabotage it?
- Will this nourish the life I'm building—or distract from it?

Proceed (or Pivot).
Make a choice—not from pressure, but from peace.

Practical Application: Redesigning One Area of Your Life

Choose one area (schedule, relationships, health, work) and redesign it from the inside out.

Ask:

- What's not working?
- What do I actually want or need?
- What's one boundary or shift I can make this week?

Let the small changes lead you back to yourself.

Mind-Body-Spirit Practice: "Aligned Yes / Aligned No"

Take a deep breath. Place your hand over your heart.

- Ask: *What is one thing I need to say "no" to this week?*
- Ask: *What is one thing I want to say a bold "yes" to, even if it scares me?*

Speak them out loud. Practice living from intention—not obligation.

Emotional Resilience: Letting Go of the Life That's No Longer Yours

Sometimes alignment requires grief. You may need to let go of a role, a rhythm, or a relationship that once felt right—but no longer serves your becoming.

That doesn't make you selfish. It makes you *spiritually honest*.

You are not abandoning the past. You're honoring your evolution.

Let yourself grow.

Jasmine's Life Rebuild

Jasmine was a community leader, wife, and mother—deeply loved but completely drained. "I looked successful on the outside," she said, "but I felt invisible on the inside."

We started with her Life Integration Map. Creativity and care were at zero. Slowly, she started painting again. Walking without her phone. Saying no to draining commitments. Within weeks, she felt alive again. "For the first time in years, my life feels like *me*."

That's alignment.

Sustainable Change: Create a Life You Can Grow Into

You don't need to create a perfect life. You need one you can *breathe* in. One that honors your healing, supports your peace, and adapts as you grow.

Design Your Life Check-In (Monthly):

- What's life-giving?

- What's draining me?

- What needs to shift so I can stay rooted in peace and truth?

Community Engagement: #MyAlignedLife

Share one aligned decision, one boundary, or one area you're redesigning. Use **#MyAlignedLife** to encourage others who are doing the brave, holy work of building lives that reflect their values—not their pressure.

You don't have to build a life that impresses others.
You're allowed to build a life that *feels like home.*

One aligned "yes" at a time.
One honest "no" at a time.
One holy decision at a time.

You're not starting over.
You're coming home—to yourself, and to God.

Reflection Questions

1. What parts of your life currently feel out of alignment?

2. What are the core values that matter most to you in this season?

3. How can your daily rhythms reflect those values more honestly?

4. Where have you been building based on fear, expectation, or pressure?

5. What would it look like to begin designing a life that feels like peace, presence, and purpose?

You weren't created to perform life.
You were created to **live it**—on purpose, from the inside out.

And when you begin to build from your truth, not just your to-do list...
When you design from your soul, not just survival...
You won't just look successful.
You'll feel whole.

And that, friend, is the life God has always invited you into.

Prayer to Build a Life That Feels Like You

God, I've built my life around so many things—
Expectations, roles, responsibilities, fear.

But I want to come back to the center.
To build from truth.
To build from alignment.

Show me where I've drifted from who You made me to be.
Give me courage to release what no longer reflects me.

I don't want a life that looks perfect.
I want a life that feels like peace.

Let my days reflect my values.
Let my rhythms reflect Your heart.
Let my choices reflect the person You're helping me become.

I trust that You are the builder—and I am safe in Your hands. Amen.

Section 4: The Becoming Never Ends – Staying Aligned as You Grow

Chapter 10: When You Outgrow Who You Were

"You're not falling apart. You're being remade."

There comes a moment in the journey of healing and alignment when you pause, look around, and realize:

I'm not who I used to be.

You may not even recognize yourself in certain spaces anymore.
The old patterns don't fit. The old conversations don't interest you.
The people who once defined your world feel... distant.

You've changed.
And while part of you might feel relieved—another part might feel disoriented.
You may even ask: *Is something wrong with me?*

Let me reassure you, as your chaplain and fellow traveler on this path:

Nothing is wrong with you.
You're not breaking down. You're *breaking through*.
You are not falling apart. You are being *remade*.

The Often-Ignored Part of Healing: Letting Go

We talk a lot about becoming whole.
We celebrate clarity, alignment, and growth.
But what's often overlooked is what must be *released* in the process.

- The version of you who lived for others' approval.
- The one who kept the peace at the expense of your own voice.
- The identity that was shaped by trauma instead of truth.
- The roles you once needed to survive but no longer serve.

You are not just stepping into new awareness.
You're shedding old versions of yourself.
And shedding—even when it's right—can feel like grief.

Because you're not just evolving—you're *saying goodbye*.
And goodbyes, even sacred ones, still carry sadness.

It's Not Regression. It's Transition.

When you're in the in-between—no longer who you were, but not yet fully who you're becoming—it's easy to mistake transition for failure.

You might feel:

- Exhausted.
- Uncertain.
- Unmotivated.
- Misunderstood.

But this is not regression.
This is *transformation*.
This is the cocoon before the wings.

In spiritual direction, we call this the *liminal space*—the holy in-between, where the old has been stripped away but the new hasn't fully taken form.

It's uncomfortable. Vulnerable. Raw.
But it's where God does His deepest work.

Outgrowing Is Not Rejection

Sometimes we confuse outgrowing with betrayal.

We think:

- "If I leave this relationship, I'm being disloyal."

- "If I no longer resonate with this environment, I'm ungrateful."

- "If I speak differently now, I'm being fake."

But outgrowing doesn't mean you've rejected your past.
It means you've *evolved beyond it*.

You can bless the old version of you and still release her.
You can honor what got you here—and still choose to walk a different path now.

Growth doesn't mean you were wrong.
It just means you're becoming more *you*.

The Emotional Toll of Transformation

Let's talk about what this actually feels like.

Growth is often marketed as clean, empowering, and exciting.
But real growth? It's usually messier.

- **You may feel confused.**
  Your values have shifted. Your energy has changed. What used to make sense doesn't anymore.

- **You may feel grief.**
  Even when you're growing in the right direction, it's hard to let go of what was familiar.

- **You may feel resistance.**
  Part of you might long to go back to what was predictable—even if it was misaligned—because it felt safe.

- **You may feel alone.**
  As you evolve, the people you once aligned with may not understand who you're becoming.

This is all normal.
More than that—it's sacred.

The Shedding Is Holy

There's a reason the metaphors of birth and resurrection are used so often in Scripture.

God is not in the business of tweaking. He's in the business of *transforming*.

> "Therefore, if anyone is in Christ, the new creation has come: The old has gone, the new is here!"
> (2 Corinthians 5:17)

Becoming new means *letting go of old*.
That means:

- Old mindsets.

- Old labels.

- Old narratives.

- Old identities that were rooted in fear, survival, or others' expectations.

Shedding these things doesn't mean you're abandoning yourself.
It means you're *finding your way back* to your truest self—the one God always saw, even when you didn't.

When You Can't Go Back

Once you've tasted wholeness, you can't pretend brokenness fits you anymore.
Once you've felt alignment, dysfunction starts to feel unbearable.
Once you've experienced clarity, confusion becomes too loud to ignore.

And yet, even with all that awareness, it can be tempting to go back—to shrink, to silence yourself, to slip back into roles that felt safer.

But here's the truth:
You can't go back. Not because you're ungrateful. But because you're not the same.

You've outgrown the skin you once wore.
Now it's time to walk in the strength you've cultivated.

Making Peace With Who You Were

It's easy to look back at old versions of yourself with embarrassment or judgment.

But I want to invite you into something different: **compassion**.

- That version of you was doing the best you could.
- You held the line when no one else did.
- You protected you when you were vulnerable.
- You kept you going when you were tired.
- You adapted to environments that didn't make space for your wholeness.

You don't need to shame yourself. You can *bless* yourself.

Say thank you.
And then say goodbye.

Because now?
Now you're walking in truth, not performance.
Now you're building a life that feels like peace, not pressure.
Now you're choosing alignment, not approval.

That is holy. And so are you, because He is Holy.

Making Room for the New

So what does it actually look like to live into this new version of you?

Here are a few practices that can support you in this sacred evolution:

---

1. Create Space to Mourn What's Ending

Grief isn't just about death. It's about change.

- Mourn the friendships that don't feel aligned anymore.

- Mourn the dream that no longer excites you.

- Mourn the identity you outgrew—even if it was once your anchor.

Give yourself permission to *feel* the loss.
Because grief, when processed with God, clears space for *new life*.

---

2. Speak the New You Into the World

Let your language shift.

- "I used to believe ___. Now I'm learning ___."
- "I'm no longer available for ___. I'm making space for ___."
- "This version of me is choosing ___. Not because I have to—because I *can*."

Your voice is part of your becoming.
Use it to declare who you're becoming, even if your hands are still shaking.

---

3. Let Your Rhythms Reflect Your Renewal

Change your habits to match the person you're becoming.

- Adjust your schedule.
- Reevaluate your commitments.
- Let your wardrobe, your surroundings, even your social spaces reflect your evolution.

This isn't superficial.
It's *symbolic*.
It's a way of signaling to your mind, your body, and your spirit: *I'm new here. And I'm allowed to act like it.*

---

4. Find Safe Spaces for the New You to Breathe

Not everyone can hold the new you. And that's okay.

You need people who won't try to drag you back to who you were.

- People who ask real questions.

- People who cheer for your growth, not just your performance.

- People who understand that evolution doesn't always look polished—and love you anyway.

You don't need a crowd. You need a circle.
Protect your space accordingly.

---

5. Let God Reintroduce You to Yourself

There are parts of you even you haven't met yet.
Parts that were buried under trauma, silenced by fear, or shamed into submission.

But God has always seen them.
And now, in this new season, He wants to reintroduce you to yourself.

Ask Him:

- What do You see in me that I've missed?

- What part of me is ready to emerge now?

- Who am I becoming—and how can I make space for that?

"Forget the former things; do not dwell on the past. See, I am doing a new thing!"
(Isaiah 43:18-19)

You Are Safe to Become

You don't have to go back.
You don't have to shrink to be loved.
You don't have to keep apologizing for changing.

You are not broken for outgrowing who you were.
You are evolving.
And that evolution is not a threat to your faith—it's a *testament to it*.

You trusted God enough to change.
Now trust Him enough to stay changed.

Normalizing Identity Shifts, Growing Pains, and Spiritual Evolution

We live in a world that celebrates clarity and confidence—but often has no language for *transition*. But the truth is, you're allowed to be in-between.

You're allowed to not fully know who you are right now.
You're allowed to feel grief for old versions of yourself.
You're allowed to evolve slowly, imperfectly, and sacredly.

Spiritual growth is not linear. It doesn't move in straight lines or tidy categories. It's cyclical, layered, and often quiet. One day you feel anchored.

The next day you're questioning everything. That's not failure. That's *formation*.

Inner Exploration: What Version of Me Am I Releasing?

Create space for stillness. Open your journal. Ask:

- What identity or role no longer feels true to who I am becoming?
- What version of me was created to survive, but isn't needed anymore?
- What am I grieving—and what am I making room for?

Be honest. Be gentle. Growth requires both.

Self-Assessment: Identity Shift Check-In

Reflect on the following statements and rate from 1 (Rarely) to 5 (Often):

1. I feel disconnected from roles that once defined me.
2. I hesitate to express new parts of myself because others expect the old me.
3. I miss who I used to be—even though I know I've outgrown that version.
4. I feel like I'm in-between identities—no longer who I was, not yet who I'm becoming.
5. I'm scared that changing will distance me from people I care about.

Scoring:

- **5–10:** You may be sensing subtle shifts—begin to give yourself language and permission.

- **11–18:** You're actively in transition—honor the tension and grieve what needs releasing.

- **19–25:** You're experiencing a full identity transformation—be deeply compassionate with yourself.

Letting Go of Roles and Identities That No Longer Serve

Your old roles were not failures. They got you here. But now, they may no longer reflect the truth of who you are.

You don't need to demonize your past to step into your future.

Instead, try this:

- **Honor:** What did this role or identity teach me?

- **Bless:** What did it protect me from? How did it help me survive or succeed?

- **Release:** What part of this identity no longer serves who I'm becoming?

This is spiritual maturity—being grateful for your past while not being bound by it.

Spiritual Care Practice: Grieve and Bless Your Past Self

Try this guided ritual:

1. Light a candle.

2. On one side of a paper, write: *"Who I Was"*—include roles, labels, and expectations you're releasing.

3. On the other side, write: *"Who I'm Becoming"*—include values, truth, or vision you're stepping into.

4. Read both sides out loud. Bless the former. Welcome the latter.

5. Tear or burn the paper, symbolizing release and rebirth.

This is not just an exercise. It's a spiritual shift.

Mind-Body-Spirit Practice: Grounding in Transition

When you feel disoriented or emotionally raw, use this somatic prayer:

1. Sit or stand with your feet grounded.

2. Place your hands on your heart and belly.

3. Breathe in: *"God, hold all that I'm letting go..."*

4. Breathe out: *"...and all that I'm becoming."*

Repeat for 3–5 minutes. Let your body feel the truth: you are safe to grow.

Emotional Resilience: You Can Grieve and Grow at the Same Time

It's okay to miss who you were and still know that she's not coming with you.

You can feel sadness and celebration in the same breath. That's what it means to evolve with grace.

Give yourself permission to:

- Cry over what you're leaving
- Mourn what's no longer a fit
- Feel lonely while you realign

There is no shame in grieving a version of you that got tired. That role served you. It protected you. But now it's time for something new.

Tasha's Unfolding

Tasha had been an executive leader in her field for over a decade. She was respected, depended on, and deeply burned out. "I don't know who I am if I'm not 'CEO Tasha,'" she whispered through tears.

She didn't want to quit. She wanted to return to herself.

Through prayer, therapy, and honest reflection, she began stepping out of over-responsibility and into rhythm. She rediscovered forgotten dreams. She gave herself permission to not always have the answers. "I thought letting go would mean losing everything," she said. "But I actually found myself."

Sustainable Change: Becoming Again and Again

You don't have to have it all figured out to take the next step. You just need the courage to *keep becoming*.

Try This Monthly Practice: Identity Check-In

Ask:

- What part of me is trying to emerge right now?

- What role or rhythm no longer fits who I'm becoming?

- What small action can I take to honor my next chapter?

Growth doesn't mean rushing. It means returning. And returning. And returning again.

Community Engagement: #WhoIAmBecoming

Share a truth, ritual, or reflection that honors who you're becoming. Use the hashtag **#WhoIAmBecoming** to affirm the sacredness of your evolution and encourage others walking through their own transformation.

You are not broken because you've changed.
You're not unstable because you're shedding old roles.
You're not lost—you're *becoming*.

Again and again, you are being remade.
Let go.
Make room.
Welcome the next version of you—with gentleness and grace.

Reflection Questions

1. What version of yourself have you outgrown—but haven't yet released?

2. What emotions are surfacing as you enter this new season?

3. What mindsets or roles are no longer aligned with who you are becoming?

4. Who are the people in your life that can hold space for your evolution?

5. What would it look like to bless your past—and boldly embrace your future?

You are not who you were—and that is a *blessing*, not a burden.

You are shedding what no longer fits so that you can walk freely, fully, and faithfully into who you were always meant to be.

You are not falling apart.
You are being *remade*.
And what's forming is more beautiful than you can yet imagine.

Prayer for the Becoming

God, I'm not who I was.
And while I don't fully know who I'm becoming,
I know that You are with me in the in-between.

Thank You for the version of me that got me here.
Thank You for her strength, her survival, her tenacity.

And now, I release her—with love.

I'm ready to be remade.
I'm ready to evolve.
I'm ready to walk in the fullness of who You've called me to be.

Even if I'm unsure, even if it's uncomfortable—
I say yes.
To this new beginning.
To this deeper becoming.
To this holy work of wholeness.

Amen.

Chapter 11: Integration Over Perfection

"Becoming whole isn't about doing it perfectly. It's about learning to return."

By now, you've done the deep work.

You've named the parts of you that were buried under performance.
You've reclaimed your voice, clarified your values, faced your pain, and started building a life that feels like *you* again.

You've experienced the power of alignment.
You've tasted the freedom that comes from living your truth.
And maybe, for the first time in a long time, you've felt at home in your own skin.

But now comes the real test—the part that isn't flashy, but is absolutely foundational:
Can you return to alignment when life inevitably pulls you out of it?

That's what this chapter is about.
Not the breakthrough. Not the "aha" moment.
But the practice of **returning**—again and again—to the truth of who you are.

Integration: The Work After the Work

So often, we treat healing as a finish line.
As if once we've uncovered the wound, named the pattern, or rewritten the belief, the work is done.

But healing isn't a single moment—it's a *movement*.
And that movement continues through **integration**.

Integration is the process of weaving everything you've learned into the fabric of your real life.

It's how your insight becomes *embodiment*.
How your values become *habits*.
How your wholeness becomes *sustainable*.

It's not about perfection.
It's about rhythm.
It's about learning how to live your truth—not once, but over time.

Why Perfection Isn't the Goal

Let's get one thing clear: **perfection is a trap**.

- Perfection says, "You can only be aligned if everything is in place."

- Integration says, "You can return to alignment—even when everything is messy."

Perfection keeps you performing.
Integration keeps you connected.

Perfection fuels shame when you fall off track.
Integration offers grace and says, *"Let's begin again."*

You weren't created to maintain a flawless life.
You were created to live a faithful one.

And faithfulness, especially to your own healing, is about returning to truth—*daily*, *compassionately*, and *imperfectly*.

The Power of Return

If you remember nothing else from this chapter, let it be this:

> **Wholeness isn't found in never drifting. It's found in always returning.**

The return is the rhythm.
The return is the redemption.
The return is the real-life practice of living in alignment, not just dreaming about it.

Because yes, life will get loud again.
Old patterns might resurface.
Stress will knock. Distractions will flood in. Unexpected loss or joy or transition will shift your rhythm.

But the difference now?

You *know the way back*.
You know the feeling of alignment.
You know how to pause, breathe, recalibrate, and return.

And that is everything.

Building a Life That Holds Your Wholeness

Integration isn't about working harder.
It's about designing your life in a way that *holds space* for your alignment.

You don't have to force your wholeness to stay.
You *make room* for it to keep returning.

Here's how.

---

1. Create Anchoring Rhythms

Rhythms are the spiritual scaffolding of our lives.
They hold us up when we're tired.
They carry us back when we've wandered.

Think of rhythms as the *habits that return you to yourself.*

- Morning stillness before the day starts

- Weekly Sabbath or tech-free rest periods

- Prayer walks or journaling check-ins

- Monthly reevaluation of your calendar and capacity

- Evening reflections or gratitude rituals

These don't need to be elaborate.
They need to be *honest*.
Rooted in what helps you feel most centered, most grounded, and most connected to God and your true self.

The goal isn't to get it "right."
The goal is to stay *rooted*.

---

2. Practice Real-Life Alignment

Your healing is not for the mountaintop moments—it's for the kitchen table. The meeting. The phone call. The interruption. The tension. The decision.

Integration asks:

- Can you hold your boundaries when it's uncomfortable?

- Can you choose rest when everything says "hustle"?

- Can you stay present in conversations that would've triggered old defenses?

- Can you speak up even when your voice shakes?

- Can you walk away when peace says, *"This is no longer yours to hold"*?

This is where your growth takes root.
Not in theory, but in *real time*.

You don't need to be perfect here.
Just *present* and *willing*.

---

3. Check in With Your Alignment Often

Don't wait for burnout or breakdown to recalibrate.
Make regular alignment check-ins part of your life rhythm.

Here are a few reflection questions you can ask weekly—or even daily:

- What feels heavy right now? What might need to be released?

- Where am I saying "yes" out of fear, not faith?

- Am I operating from truth or from an old narrative?

- What is my body trying to tell me?

- Where is God inviting me to return to peace, presence, or purpose?

Integration isn't passive. It's *attentive*.
It's about noticing misalignment early and gently making your way back.

---

4. Build Supportive Environments

Your environment can either support your alignment—or sabotage it.

Take inventory of the spaces and relationships you occupy:

- Do they make space for your healing, or do they keep you performing?

- Do your surroundings reflect your values?

- Are you surrounding yourself with people who celebrate your growth—or pull you back into old roles?

Integration becomes easier when you're not doing it alone.
Build environments—internally and externally—that reflect who you're becoming.

---

5. Let Grace Carry You Forward

There will be days you forget everything you've learned.
Days when old habits take over.
When the voices of shame get loud again.
When you feel like you've regressed instead of progressed.

Those moments are not proof that your healing didn't "stick."
They're proof that you're *human*.

> "My grace is sufficient for you, for my power is made perfect in weakness."
> *(2 Corinthians 12:9)*

Let grace meet you there.
Let it carry you—not back to square one, but into deeper trust, deeper surrender, deeper *return*.

The Rhythm of Becoming

Integration is not linear.
It looks more like this:

- Alignment

- Drift

- Return

- Reset

- Repeat

And every time you return, you don't just come back to where you were.
You come back with more *awareness*, more *compassion*, more *resilience*.

You're not repeating.
You're *reinforcing* your wholeness with every return.

This is the rhythm of becoming.
This is what it means to live in integrity with your healing.

What Integration *Feels* Like

As you practice this rhythm, you may notice subtle but powerful shifts:

- You recover more quickly from emotional spirals.

- You recognize old patterns sooner—and choose differently.

- You trust your own discernment more deeply.

- You protect your peace more consistently.

- You embody your truth more naturally.

This is what real growth looks like.
Not perfection—but *presence*.
Not unshakable certainty—but *faithful return*.

A Life You Can Sustain

Ultimately, this is about creating a life that doesn't just *look* whole—but *feels* sustainable.

A life where your wholeness isn't dependent on mood, momentum, or other people's expectations.

But is supported by rhythms, habits, and grace that bring you back—again and again—to center.

You don't have to prove anything.
You just have to *practice coming home* to yourself.

How to Stay Rooted When Life Gets Loud Again

The truth is, the world won't stop being chaotic just because you've started healing. Your inbox won't stay empty. Your relationships won't always reflect your growth. But you now have something you didn't before: *tools* and *truths* to return to.

Staying rooted doesn't mean you never get overwhelmed. It means you know how to find your way back.

- Back to stillness.

- Back to your breath.

- Back to your God.

- Back to yourself.

That's integration—bringing the truth into your *everyday reality*.

Inner Exploration: What Pulls Me Out of Alignment Most Often?

Sit with God and reflect:

- When do I most often abandon my practices or peace?

- What does "getting off track" look like for me?

- What would it look like to return—gently, consistently, and without shame?

This awareness becomes your roadmap for staying connected.

Self-Assessment: Integration Inventory

Rate from 1 (Strongly Disagree) to 5 (Strongly Agree):

1. I notice quickly when I've drifted from my center.

2. I have regular rhythms that help me return to alignment.

3. I respond to setbacks with grace, not shame.

4. I check in with myself spiritually, emotionally, and physically.

5. I adjust my strategies as my season of life shifts.

Scoring:

- **5–10:** Begin with simple rituals of return—your soul is asking for support.

- **11–18:** You're building a life that holds your growth—refine your rhythms.

- **19–25:** You're living your truth consistently—protect it with grace and structure.

Embracing Cyclical Growth and Spiritual Maintenance

Growth is not a straight line. It's a spiral. A return. A deepening. You will revisit old wounds, patterns, and doubts. But now, you'll meet them *differently.*

You'll meet them with tools.
With presence.
With compassion.
With God.

Think of your spiritual life like a garden. It needs:

- **Water** – daily practices that nourish your soul

- **Weeding** – honest reflection and adjustment

- **Rest** – time to just be, without needing to perform

- **Light** – community, connection, and grace

Your growth deserves maintenance, not perfectionism.

Practical Application: Monthly Check-Ins + Seasonal Resets

Monthly Check-In Questions:

- Where did I feel most aligned this month?

- What practices supported my peace?

- What drained me or distracted me from myself?

- What is one rhythm I want to recommit to next month?

Seasonal Reset Practice:

- Choose a quiet morning or afternoon.

- Journal or pray through:

    - *What am I carrying that I need to release?*

    - *What is God inviting me to embrace in this new season?*

- Set one focus word or intention to guide the next few months.

Integration doesn't require a full overhaul—just consistent *honest check-ins*.

Mind-Body-Spirit Practice: "Return to Center" Breath Prayer

Use this anytime you feel scattered or overwhelmed.

1. Inhale: *"God, ground me in what's true..."*

2. Exhale: *"...and bring me back to center."*

Repeat for 2–5 minutes. Let your nervous system learn that alignment is always accessible.

Emotional Resilience: When You Feel Like You're Slipping Backward

It will happen. Life will throw something unexpected. You'll fall out of rhythm. An old pattern might resurface. And your inner critic will whisper, *"You're losing it. You're not really whole."*

Here's the truth: **You're not starting over. You're deepening.**

The evidence of growth is not that you never fall—it's that you *notice sooner and return quicker.* That's resilience. That's integration.

When you mess up, don't spiral. Return.

When you're tired, don't push. Pause.

When you feel disconnected, don't withdraw. Reconnect.

Malik's Integration Journey

Malik had done deep soul work. He'd realigned his values and restructured his life. But one month, work picked up, family life got overwhelming, and his practices slipped. "I started spiraling," he said. "But then I realized—I know how to return."

He didn't shame himself. He paused, prayed, and reintroduced one simple rhythm: 10 minutes of stillness each morning.

"That alone brought me back," he shared. "Integration isn't about doing everything perfectly. It's about staying close enough to notice when you're drifting—and having the courage to come home."

Sustainable Change: Protecting What You've Built

Integration is about creating scaffolding—rituals, relationships, and rhythms that *hold your alignment* even when life changes.

Three Tools for Long-Term Integration:

1. **Daily Anchor Practices**

    - Choose 1–2 habits that ground you each day (ex: breath prayer, morning journaling, evening stillness).

2. **Weekly Reflection**

    - End each week with this question: *Where did I live aligned? Where did I abandon myself?*

3. **Quarterly Reset**

    - Schedule a "retreat" morning or afternoon every 3 months—reassess, rest, and realign.

Community Engagement: #ReturnToCenter

For one week, share a daily moment where you noticed yourself returning—whether through breath, prayer, boundaries, or pause. Use the hashtag **#ReturnToCenter** to remind others (and yourself) that grace is always available.

You weren't called to live a flawless life.
You were called to live a *faithful* one.
Not perfect. But *present*.
Not polished. But *anchored*.

You are allowed to drift.
You are allowed to pause.
And you are always allowed to *return*.

Integration isn't about getting it all right.
It's about staying connected to what's real.
To what's true.
To what's *you*.

Let's keep returning—again and again.

Reflection Questions

1. What does "returning to alignment" look like for you in real life?

2. Where are you still chasing perfection instead of practicing integration?

3. What daily or weekly rhythms help you stay rooted in your truth?

4. What environments (physical, relational, or spiritual) need to shift to support your continued healing?

5. How can you show yourself more grace when you feel out of sync?

Wholeness isn't a destination. It's a rhythm.

It's not about never getting distracted.
It's about always coming back.

To your center.
To your values.
To your truth.
To God.

You don't need to be perfect.
You just need to keep returning.

And that return? That is what makes you whole.

A Prayer for Integration

God, I've done so much work to heal, align, and return.
And now I ask You—help me sustain it.

Not through perfection, but through presence.
Not through pressure, but through practice.

Teach me to notice when I drift.
And give me the courage to return.

Let my rhythms reflect Your grace.
Let my routines reflect my values.
Let my life reflect who I'm becoming in You.

When I forget, remind me.
When I fall short, catch me.
When I grow weary, restore me.

I don't want to perform wholeness.
I want to *live* it.
One imperfect, grace-filled step at a time.

Amen.

Chapter 12: Living Authentically in Real Life

"You don't have to pretend to be holy. You already are whole."

You've come a long way.

You've named the ache.
You've unmasked the false self.
You've faced your hidden wounds with compassion.
You've let go of roles that once kept you safe but no longer fit.
You've learned to listen inward, rest deeply, speak truthfully, and return—again and again—to the sacred center of your being.

Now comes the most sacred, and perhaps the most vulnerable, part of the journey:

Can you live this in real life?

Not just in your journal.
Not just in your prayers.
Not just when you're alone with God.

But in your *home*.
In your *marriage*.
In your *friendships*, your *calling*, your *work*, your *worship*, your *conflict*, your *daily rhythms*.

Can you be whole in a world that rewards performance?

Because that's where healing is tested.
And that's also where healing becomes real.

The Shift from Healing to Living

There's something beautifully safe about the inner work.
Even though it's hard and often painful, there's a kind of sacred privacy to it.

It's one thing to feel whole in silence and stillness.
It's another thing entirely to walk into a room and *remain whole*.

To carry your truth into spaces where you once abandoned it.
To embody your values in places that once required you to shrink.
To speak from alignment in environments that still want your performance.

This chapter isn't about changing the world.
It's about choosing to remain **true to yourself** as you live in it.

Authenticity Is Not a Trend

In our culture, the word "authenticity" is everywhere.
It's on T-shirts and social media captions.
It's used as branding. A vibe. A trend.

But in the spiritual life, authenticity is not a buzzword.
It's a **posture**.

It's the moment-by-moment decision to:

- Be honest instead of polished.

- Be real instead of perfect.

- Be grounded instead of impressive.

- Be led by God, not shaped by pressure.

Authenticity is the spiritual courage to say, *"This is who I am—because this is who God made me to be."*

And to *live* from that place, not occasionally—but **daily**.

The Risk of Being Real

Let's not sugarcoat it: being authentic has a cost.

When you start living as your whole self:

- Some people may not understand you anymore.

- Some spaces may feel misaligned.

- Some expectations may need to be broken.

- Some applause may go quiet.

But here's what I've learned:

> The cost of *not* being real is far greater.

When you trade your truth for acceptance, you lose both.
When you perform to belong, you betray yourself to fit in.
And when you silence your soul to keep the peace, you forfeit the deep peace that only comes through alignment.

But when you live authentically?
You don't just find clarity—you find *God*.

Because He meets you—not in the image you curate—but in the *truth* of who you are.

What Does Authenticity Look Like in Real Life?

Let's get practical.
Living authentically doesn't mean you bare your soul to everyone, everywhere.
It means you stop abandoning your truth to manage perception or meet unrealistic expectations.

Here's what it might look like:

---

1. At Work

You stop over-explaining your boundaries.
You stop chasing validation through over-performance.
You start honoring your pace and trusting your voice—even when others don't get it.
You speak up when something feels wrong.
You stop striving to be the "ideal" leader, team member, or employee—and start being *honest, present, and whole*.

2. In Relationships

You choose connection over control.
You let people see your vulnerability instead of pretending to always be strong.
You stop editing your truth to avoid discomfort.
You give love and receive love as the real you—not the "pleaser" or the "fixer" or the "predictable one."
You start saying, *"This is what I need"* instead of *"Whatever works for you."*

3. In Parenting

You show your kids that wholeness is possible—even when you mess up.
You model rest, boundaries, and self-compassion.
You stop performing as the perfect parent and start becoming the *present* one.
You let your children see what it looks like to come home to yourself—and to God.

4. In Ministry or Faith Communities

You stop pretending to be more "together" than you are.
You stop hiding your questions, your burnout, or your grief.
You let your faith be both bold and honest.
You refuse to trade spiritual performance for sacred presence.

Authenticity in faith is not a lack of reverence—it's the *most reverent thing you can offer*: your *real* self to a *real* God.

Holiness Isn't a Performance—It's Presence

Somewhere along the way, we learned to perform "holy."
To curate the right tone. To say the right words. To show up polished and ready.

But holiness isn't found in pretending.
Holiness is found in *presence*.

- In the woman who stops mid-task to breathe and remember she is held.

- In the parent who chooses patience over perfection.

- In the leader who admits they don't have the answers.

- In the friend who says, "I don't need to fix you. I just want to be with you."

- In the believer who prays, not to impress, but to connect.

You don't have to *earn* your holiness.
You already carry it—because God *dwells within you*.

You are holy—not because you perform well, but because you are *whole* in Him.

Living in the Light of Who You Are

> "But everything exposed by the light becomes visible—and everything that is illuminated becomes a light."
> *(Ephesians 5:13)*

Living authentically is living in the *light*.
Not in fear of exposure—but in *freedom*.

When you stop hiding...
When you stop striving...
When you stop managing other people's perception of you...

You become *light* for others.

You become the safe space where others can show up real, too.
You become the quiet presence that helps others drop the mask.
You become the proof that wholeness is possible—not because life is perfect, but because *you're no longer pretending*.

The Legacy of Wholeness

As you continue walking this journey, remember:
The goal isn't to impress.
It's to *embody*.
To live from a place of truth, grace, and love.

That's the kind of life that transforms not just you—but the world around you.

Because when people encounter someone who is truly whole:

- They don't feel intimidated.

- They feel *invited*.

- Invited to exhale.

- Invited to rest.

- Invited to return to themselves and to God.

That's your legacy—not what you build, but *who you become*.

You Already Carry What You Need

There's no next level to unlock.
No higher version of you to chase.

You already carry everything you need for the life God's calling you to live.

You don't have to perform to be accepted.
You don't have to hustle to be loved.
You don't have to strive to be seen.

You *are* loved.
You *are* seen.
You *are* whole.

Now...
Live like it.

Being Whole in a Fractured World

The world is noisy, distracted, and disoriented. And it will try to make you feel the same way.

But as someone who has done the inner work, you now carry something precious: *clarity. Alignment. Peace.* And that peace is not just for you—it's meant to be *lived*, shared, and embodied.

Living authentically doesn't mean your life looks flawless. It means your life reflects your *truth*.

Wholeness in real life looks like:

- Saying no when your peace is at stake

- Asking for help without shame

- Holding your boundaries with love

- Showing up real, not perfect

- Choosing presence over pressure

- Trusting that *God will meet you in your honesty, not your performance*

Inner Exploration: What Does Authenticity Look Like for Me Now?

In stillness or journaling, ask yourself:

- Where in my life do I still feel pressure to perform or please?

- What feels the most "me" right now?

- What part of myself do I want to show the world more of?

- What does it mean for me to live whole—even when others don't understand?

Let your soul answer. This is your sacred truth.

Self-Assessment: Authenticity in Action

Rate from 1 (Rarely) to 5 (Often):

1. I speak the truth in love, even when it's uncomfortable.

2. I don't over-explain or shrink who I am to make others more comfortable.

3. My daily choices reflect my deepest values and beliefs.

4. I show up consistently as my true self—in public and in private.

5. I release the need to be perfect in order to be loved.

Scoring:

- **5–10:** You're awakening to your truth—start small, stay consistent.

- **11–18:** You're living more authentically—protect it as you grow.

- **19–25:** You're embodying wholeness—stay rooted, and help others do the same.

Walking in Alignment When Others Don't Get It

Let's be honest—your wholeness may confuse people who benefited from your people-pleasing. Your peace may disrupt systems built on striving. Your boundaries may challenge dynamics where you used to bend.

That's okay.

You don't need everyone's agreement to live in alignment.
You just need your own *integrity*.
And your peace is proof that you're on the right path.

Remember:

- You're not required to stay small to keep others comfortable.

- You're not selfish for living from your values.

- You're not wrong for evolving—even if others stay the same.

Practical Application: Your Authentic Living Manifesto

Take time this week to write your own "authenticity manifesto." A living document that declares how you will show up, from this day forward.

Include affirmations like:

- I will not abandon myself to be accepted.

- I will pause and listen to my soul before saying yes.

- I will honor my voice, my values, and my pace.

- I will trust that God meets me in truth, not performance.

Read it aloud. Revisit it often. Let it guide your decisions.

Mind-Body-Spirit Practice: "I Am Whole" Grounding Ritual

Use this anytime you feel the pull to perform or shrink.

1. Sit or stand with your spine straight and feet grounded.

2. Close your eyes. Place your hand over your heart.

3. Inhale slowly: *"I am enough."*

4. Exhale slowly: *"I am whole."*

5. Repeat: *"I do not have to hustle to be holy. I am already held."*

Let your body internalize your wholeness. Not as a concept, but as *truth*.

Emotional Resilience: The Courage to Keep Showing Up Real

Living authentically will stretch you. There will be moments where you're tempted to perform again. Where the fear of rejection rises. Where you wonder if it's safer to go back.

But hear this: **wholeness is worth the risk.**

You will find your people. You will attract what aligns. You will experience peace not because life is easy, but because *you are no longer hiding*.

Stay the course. Your real self is your *free* self.

Jennifer's Unveiling

Jennifer was an executive, respected in ministry and leadership circles. But deep down, she felt like she was wearing a mask. "I didn't even know how to access my true self anymore," she said.

Through soul care and alignment work, she began to notice where she was shrinking, pleasing, and hiding. Slowly, she removed the mask. She said no when she needed to. She started journaling again. She showed up messy in conversations—and was still loved.

"I thought I had to earn belonging," she said. "But I've never felt more seen than when I stopped performing."

That's authenticity. That's peace.

Sustainable Change: Stay Rooted, Stay Real

You don't need a dramatic transformation to live authentically. You just need a consistent return to your truth.

Weekly Authenticity Check-In:

- Where did I abandon myself this week?

- Where did I show up true?

- What do I need to reaffirm to stay aligned?

Let this be your rhythm—not judgment, but joy.

Community Engagement: #LivingAuthentically

Share your manifesto, your reflections, or one aligned decision that made you feel more like *you*. Use the hashtag **#LivingAuthentically** to inspire others and witness the beauty of this brave, holy way of being.

You don't have to pretend to be at peace.
You don't have to try harder to be whole.
You are already everything God created you to be.
And now you have the tools to *live* from that place.

In public and in private.
In the spotlight and in the quiet.
In success and in stillness.

This is not the end of your journey.
It's the beginning of a life that truly feels like *yours*.

Reflection Questions

1. Where in your life do you still feel tempted to perform instead of show up authentically?

2. What would it look like to embody your wholeness in your daily relationships?

3. What part of your life has been most transformed through this journey of alignment?

4. How can you remind yourself daily that you are already whole, already holy, already loved?

5. Who in your life can support your continued commitment to living from truth—not performance?

This is the life you were made for.

Not a life of burnout, image-management, or quiet despair.
But a life of truth.
A life of rest.
A life of alignment.
A life that is *holy*—because it is *whole*.

You don't have to pretend to be holy.
You already *are*—in Him.

So take the truth you've uncovered, the healing you've walked through, and the peace you've reclaimed…

And go *live it*.
Fully.
Freely.
Authentically.
Everywhere you go.

This is not the end of your journey.
It's the beginning of a life fully lived.

A Prayer for Living Authentically

God, I've spent so long trying to be what others needed.
Trying to please, perform, protect, and produce.

But now, I want to live from the truth.
The truth that I am loved—without earning it.
That I am whole—without striving for it.

Help me carry my wholeness into real life.
Not just in prayer, but in how I show up at work.
Not just in solitude, but in how I love others.

Let me be brave enough to live as the person You made me to be.
Let me embody Your peace.
Let me reflect Your presence.

Not through perfection.
But through presence.

I don't want to perform holy.
I want to *live* whole.

Amen.

Closing: You Were Never Broken. You Were Just Disconnected

"You've always been whole. This journey simply helped you remember."

If you've made it here, you've done something sacred. You've said yes to the slow, courageous work of returning—not to a shinier version of yourself, but to your *true self*. The you God created. The you that was never lost, only buried beneath expectations, fear, and survival.

So let me say this clearly and with conviction:

You were never broken.
You were just disconnected.

Disconnected from your truth.
From your peace.
From your presence.
From your voice.
From your God.

And now, little by little, you've come back.

Not because you finally got it all together.
Not because you worked harder.
But because you finally made space to *listen*—and to *heal*.

You've Always Been Whole

You were whole before the world told you who to be.
You were whole before the trauma, the burnout, the heartbreak.
You were whole even in the moments you couldn't feel it.

This journey didn't create your wholeness.
It simply uncovered what was already there.

And now, you know how to return.
To truth.
To peace.
To yourself.
To God.

Not just once.
But over and over again.

Encouragement for the Next Chapter of Your Becoming

This book is closing, but your becoming isn't over.

There will still be days when you drift, question, or forget. But now you have tools, rhythms, and truths to return to. You've built spiritual scaffolding that can hold you in every season.

So as you move forward, remember:

- You don't have to be perfect to be powerful.

- You don't have to know everything to walk in alignment.

- You don't have to explain your peace to people who don't understand it.

- You don't have to strive for worth you already carry.

You get to walk out this life from the inside out—with love, with purpose, and with grace.

Let your wholeness be your quiet revolution.

Final Integration Exercise: A Letter to Your Future Aligned Self

Before you turn this final page, I want to invite you into one last sacred practice.

Write a letter to your future aligned self.

The version of you six months from now. A year from now. The you who has continued to choose presence over pressure, peace over perfection, and truth over performance.

Begin like this:

> *Dear Future Me,*
> I know life will still try to pull you away from your center. But here's what I want you to remember...

Include:

- The truths you've uncovered

- The values you want to protect

- The rhythms that help you feel like you

- The prayer you want to carry into your next season

- The voice of grace you want to speak over yourself again and again

Seal it. Keep it sacred. Come back to it when you need to remember who you are.

And so, dear one...

You are not behind.
You are not too much.
You are not too late.
You are not broken.

You are whole.
You are aligned.
You are becoming.

One breath, one choice, one return at a time.

May the peace of Christ meet you every time you pause.
May your truth rise louder than the noise.
And may your life always reflect the beauty of your becoming.

Let's stay connected.

I'm cheering you on—always.

— *Ivory Jamerson*
That Chaplain | Spiritual Healthcare Provider | Fellow Journeyer

About the Author

Ivory Jamerson is a clinical chaplain, a senior ministry leader, and entrepreneur pioneering a movement in spiritual healthcare. With over two decades of experience in the healing and helping professions, she is **passionate about restoring lives through alignment—spirit, soul, and body.**

As the founder of a spiritual care center and a portfolio of business ventures centered on the whole person concept, **Ivory is redefining what it means to care for individuals holistically.** She brings a bold yet compassionate voice to the intersection of faith, mental health, and physical well-being.

Ivory holds a Master of Divinity and is in the final phase of her Master of Social Work. Her work spans hospice care, addiction and recovery, trauma-informed counseling, military and family support, and leadership development. Whether speaking, writing, or consulting, **she leads with integrity, authenticity, and unwavering purpose.**

But above all, **Ivory's greatest pride and joy is her family**. She has been married to her husband, Chad, for over 20 years. Together, they are raising five beautiful children and continuing to build a life anchored in faith, love, and legacy.

Learn more at spiritualhealthcareconsulting.com
Follow the movement: **#ThatChaplain**

Notes

Notes

www.ingramcontent.com/pod-product-compliance
Lightning Source LLC
Chambersburg PA
CBHW070531090426
42735CB00013B/2945